JOURNEY OF THE BROKEN VESSELS

Copyright © 2024 by Ashten Duncan
All rights reserved.

No part of this publication may be reproduced, distributed, or transmitted in any form or by any means, including photocopying, recording, or other electronic or mechanical methods, without the publisher's prior written permission, except as permitted by U.S. copyright law.

The story, all names, characters, and incidents portrayed in this production are fictitious. No identification with actual persons (living or deceased), places, buildings, and products is intended or should be inferred.

Book Cover by Stefan Prodanovic
Edited by Shelby Perlis

ISBN: 979-8-9911957-0-6 (paperback)
ISBN: 979-8-9911957-1-3 (ebook)

First Edition: August 2024

Published by Ashten Duncan

To my wife, family, and all of my brothers and sisters in healthcare who suffer moral injury in silence.

ACKNOWLEDGMENTS

I WOULD LIKE TO GIVE SPECIAL THANKS TO MY WIFE, Elyssa Wallace, whose support of and belief in me made this novel possible. I would also like to acknowledge my parents and sister for their love and support throughout my educational journey, which recently culminated in my graduation from a residency program in family medicine.

I would like to thank the following physicians and other healthcare professionals who provided their subject-matter expertise in the form of content editing and sensitivity reading for this book: Fen Sartorius, Mac Bowen, Kristin Graziano, Isabel Díaz Morfin, Nora Kratz, Cameron Kilpatrick, Daniel Sadoway, Esther Tipton, Khuzeman Abbasi, and Madison Kajder. I would also like to thank Tenzin Yangchen and Carlos Martinez for serving as beta readers for this large-scale project.

Lastly, I would like to thank the others who helped with this work's developmental and structural editing and provided overarching feedback on the narrative. Every suggestion led to a better final product, and I am proud of what this novel ultimately became.

CHAPTER ONE

Frieden Bay

> Call it what it was: it was always a fool, always a great fool. It was not what one would call extraordinary— nor gifted. Nor revolutionary. It was not even what you would call a man. Nor a woman. Nor a thing of any pleasure.

The puissant rays of the midday sun pierced through the smudged windshield of the sedan whose driver wearily adjusted the radio's volume knob to bring the sound of the alternative rock music down to a whisper. Six hours on the main highway had lulled me into a trance where—unless I was in imminent danger of colliding with oncoming traffic or wildlife— my eyes remained glued to a point many yards ahead of me. When the exit sign for Frieden Bay became visible, I picked up my now-tepid coffee. I sipped it before exiting onto a highway, which looked as wide as any given city street in a typical suburb.

My mind drifted to what prompted this cross-country drive to Frieden Bay. In March, I received a life-changing letter: my official notice that I had matched at the family medicine residency program in a remote community on the East Coast. During my interview with this program, I was impressed by the postgraduate education they provided to trainees in this community, which encouraged autonomy in clinical decision-making and a community health approach to caring for patients. There was also the wonderful opportunity to train alongside residents in other specialties without having to compete for procedures and other forms of hands-on learning. This chance to train in such a unique place was golden for someone like me, who was not committed to one path forward.

The small local highway passed through several almost identically structured hills, with some dipping downward slightly more so than the ones before them. The undulating terrain gave brief glimpses of what lay before me, but nothing could offer a solid portrait of my destination. Although it appeared that commuters had to use this highway frequently because no others led directly to Frieden Bay, the asphalt was in immaculate condition, nearly glistening under the daylight. I shrugged at the thought of it, attributing it to excellent maintenance or design. The smoothness of the pavement provided a welcoming transition to my new residence.

I smiled as I glanced at the disorganized mess in my passenger seat. My old, frayed, brown leather laptop bag contained the various accouterments I had used since starting medical school. My dependable stethoscope, with its crimson tubing covered in the residue of countless alcohol swabs, reminded me of when I learned how to listen to a patient's lungs as a first-year student. My metal penlight, with its random scratches and dents, evoked memories of one of the neurologists whose bravado made me nervous but also ensured I never forgot how to perform a neurological exam. My little knot-tying simulator, crudely made out of a piece of twine and a paperclip, took me back to times when I would sit awake and practice my hand-tying while on call with the surgery team.

The grassy hills gave way to a clearing where I could make out the faint outlines of buildings abutting the shore of a bay. An army of daunting trees insulated the town from the rest of the area, with the only disruption in the ranks being the very highway on which I drove. Vast stretches of multicolored geraniums, lilies, and azaleas filled the land with an almost magical peace beyond the trees. Little rock outcroppings emerging from the hills decorated the expanse before me with nests of contrasting neutral colors, which reminded me of the beautiful landscape paintings that lined the halls of my college's library. Far in the distance was the gloriously sun-bathed sea, which stretched far beyond the horizon like a beautiful cerulean blanket. Time slowed momentarily, allowing me to exist in this new environment.

I hummed along to a familiar song on the radio as I gently turned my wheel in preparation for the winding path ahead. Coasting downward in a gentle and smooth spiral, I took in the awe-inspiring scenery around me once more before attending to my tasks for the day. I had been speaking with a local real estate tycoon who owned myriad properties all across the region. This person had an apartment for rent not too far away from the hospital and clinic where I would be working for the next three years. Although my feelings were mixed about adding to the wallet of someone whose coffers were already filled to the brim, I needed a convenient space for what would be a challenging phase of my professional training.

As my vehicle entered the forest that separated the serene outlying field from Frieden Bay, I peered at the clock to see that I might be late if I did not hasten my pace. The woods were different from what I had experienced back in the central part of the country: they teemed with titanic pine and oak trees, stretching their many green hands up toward the sky to create a canopy, preventing any passage of light. This entire segment of the highway felt like an enduring crepuscular vault in which the only reminder of time was the darkening to night. I rolled down my window to breathe in the fresh scent of pine needles and nearby seawater, which sliced through the otherwise eerie forest atmosphere.

The dim tunnel of the forest gave way to the brilliant environment of Frieden Bay. The hints of life I saw at a distance presented themselves in their full splendor: lovely red- and brown-brick homes with brightly colored roofs lining the shoreline. The cloudless sky above Frieden Bay was a powerful reminder of the fresh start I hoped to achieve with this move of over six hundred miles to the east. As the highway gave way to a series of smaller, tributary-like city streets, my face relaxed, and my lips curved upward with unalloyed delight. The excitement of change displaced the nervousness and reservations I had carried with me just before leaving my family and friends.

I pulled into a parking spot in front of the apartment complex's administrative building. I raised myself lazily out of the cool interior and into the warm, humid air of Frieden Bay. The sensation I got from this new environment was blissful. I deeply inhaled the saline breeze, which welcomingly caressed my unfamiliar skin. The scent of the bay was unlike any other I had experienced in my life, and yet, the administrative building seemed like many others I had seen before. After soaking in the scenery for a short time longer, I entered to meet the landlord.

The corridor to the landlord's office was unusually circuitous, with large winding walls guiding me into what seemed to be oblivion. It was as if the architects who had designed this building wanted to prevent any passersby from finding their way to what was supposed to be a place of business. The panels of wood lining the walls were painted a peculiar gray, giving the impression of walking through a vacant subway station. The monochromatic scheme of the corridor was completed by a dingy black carpet that hit me in the face with a musty odor. The carpet accentuated the gray walls, creating the illusion that the corridor was much wider than it actually was. I glanced above me to find that the fluorescent lighting was quite dim. Before that, it had not occurred to me that the dimness made the walk to the landlord's office feel like a venture into a dense fog.

I reached an enormous door that stood ten feet tall and possibly half that measurement wide. A small window rested at the door's apex, casting a thin beam of light into the otherwise caliginous corridor. I took a moment to stare at the black plaque fastened to the oak door before me. Despite the inadequate lighting, I could make out 'C. Haron – Landlord' in curious scarlet letters on the plaque. After confirming that I was in the right place, I knocked on the massive door, noting how dull the sound was when my knuckles struck it.

"Who is it?" a gravelly voice called from the other side. "Are you the new tenant, by chance?"

"Yes," I replied, half-entranced by the landlord's imposing office door. "I'm here to check in with you, Mr. Haron."

I heard shuffling on the other side of the door before it flung open, revealing an older, large man wearing a black suit with heather-gray pinstripes and an eccentrically green bowtie. Before I realized it, he firmly gripped my right hand with both of his and shook it with enough force to knock me off balance. His thin lips curled into a wide smile as he made eye contact with me.

"Come in, come in," he insisted as he gestured toward one of the two wooden chairs in front of his gargantuan desk.

I stepped into the office and settled into the chair nearer to the wall. The office—adorned with various paintings and marble sculptures—stood in stark contrast to the barren corridor that led to this surreal working space. A large window hung ajar, framing a gorgeous view of the sea. I sat quietly, taking in the unexpected comfort of the office.

"First of all, I would like to welcome you to Frieden Bay," the man grunted as he dropped himself into his charcoal-colored swivel chair. "As you may have noticed, based on the information I sent you a few months ago, Frieden Bay is home to a fairly small number of permanent residents with the occasional influx of vacationers and seasonal occupants who own some of the priciest properties right on the water. In many ways, this town is the perfect place to put down roots and become part of our tight-knit community."

"That sounds wonderful," I replied. "It's just as I imagined it would be."

"So, to get down to business," Mr. Haron said as he shuffled through his file cabinet. "No pets, I trust?"

"None whatsoever. I intended for this to be a fresh start with just me."

"I understand. A common reason for many people who join us out here."

"Frieden Bay is certainly a wonderland," I ventured after listening to the faint rustling of papers and creaking of the aluminum file cabinet.

"I know what you mean. It does have a certain quaintness to it that—if you ask me—makes it rather charming," the landlord said gruffly. "So, you're out here for work, eh?"

"That's right. I signed my employment paperwork just before making the cross-country drive. I'm one of the new family medicine resident physicians at Alta Vista Hospital and Primary Care Center."

"Excellent. Given your line of work, I can wait for your paystub with your first paycheck, which should come in the next month or so."

Mr. Haron chuckled as he pulled out a stack of stapled papers, spun around, and placed them on the desk in front of me.

He stretched across the desk to grab an antique fountain pen, placing it neatly beside the papers.

"This is the lease agreement I emailed you the other day. It's mostly standard clauses—boilerplate stuff, you know."

I picked up the documents before me and glanced at them, noting that they were identical to the electronic file on my computer. I reached for the fountain pen on the desk and noticed how smooth and almost otherworldly it felt. It was a curious pen with the same scarlet letters I saw on the black plaque etched into its side. As I pressed the pen tip against the paper, the pen seemingly did most of the work with how effortlessly it glided across each page. To my surprise, the ink was red, but this did not bother the landlord. After initialing and signing in numerous spots, Mr. Haron looked over my shoulder, nodded, and retrieved the documents.

I could not quite place why, but I felt distinctly uncomfortable as Mr. Haron reached over me to grab the papers. It felt as if I had just signed my life away—like a contract signed in blood. Perhaps it was the reality that, no matter what, I was locked into my residency program and would be in Frieden Bay for the next three years. While technically possible, switching training programs was no easy feat. Unlike in most other professions, where you could simply find a new job, you were bound to your residency training as a new, undifferentiated physician. In the United States, you were essentially unemployable without an unrestricted license and board certification in a medical specialty.

"Very good. To let you know: I will be away from the office for a few weeks for reasons I'd rather not belabor right now,"

Mr. Haron declared with a less-than-modest air of self-assurance as he deposited the signed contract into a manila file folder labeled "New Arrivals" in large red letters.

"That's no problem at all," I responded, rising from the chair. "I should be okay until you return."

With a few more quick movements, Mr. Haron gathered a set of keys, a local tour guide, and a sheet with office business hours and other pertinent information and handed them to me.

"Well, I think that pretty much covers everything," Mr. Haron stated before loudly yawning. "I have some packing to do while there's still light so I can catch a ferry. So, if you excuse me, I will be on my way."

CHAPTER TWO

Unpacking Boxes

> *It was as it would ever be: a fool in drab garments bearing no crest.*

I squinted my eyes to make out the numbers on the sides of each apartment building until I detected the faint outline of "400" a few hundred yards away from the landlord's office. After finding my designated parking space marked "402," I pulled in and sighed in relief as I noticed my unit was on the first floor. I glanced over my shoulder and realized I had much work to do for this new residence. Before dealing with the colossal task of moving everything inside, I decided it would be best to get acquainted with the living space and make mental notes about where everything should go.

The apartment building was quite aged, weathered by the coastal environment. It was built in an American Colonial-inspired style, typical of this part of the country. Clinging vines of English ivy covered the exterior walls of the buildings, adding strands of vibrant green against the beiges and grays. The staircases were well-kept wood, with metal banisters layered in slightly chipped white paint. Large trees towered above the sidewalks, casting dense shade along the paths leading to each unit.

I trod across the sweltering pavement, which sapped my energy and made me feel tired before I even started moving in. After fumbling with the new keys, I unlocked the door to the apartment. Upon entering, I immediately noticed the high ceilings and bare white walls. It was already partially furnished with some essentials. Beautiful hardwood covered the floors in most of the apartment, with white tiles in the bathroom and kitchen. Despite its age, the apartment had a cozy and inviting feel. The spacious living room had large windows overlooking a bustling street below, which infused the space with natural light. A comfortable sofa and a few eclectic pieces of furniture adorned the room, lending it a lived-in and welcoming aura.

The kitchen was small but functional, with retro appliances that added to the charm of the space. The dark granite countertops contrasted with the pale green of the walls. The sweet scent of potted flowers lingered in the air, adding to the coziness of the apartment. I could not help but feel a sense of nostalgia wash over me as I explored the different rooms of the unit. The scents, sounds, and sights transported me back to a house my family and I lived in as a child during the 2000s.

The bedroom here was simple yet elegant, with enough space for my sleigh bed to go in the middle of the room. Fresh latex paint wafted through the air and met my nostrils, evoking memories of lazy summer days when I wanted to make my bedroom feel like a skyward kingdom by painting the walls a crisp azure. A soft breeze blew through the open windows, carrying the soothing sounds of the waves crashing against the shore just east of the apartment complex. I went to the balcony connected to the bedroom, where I encountered a breathtaking view of the bay and adjoining sea. The salty sea air filled my lungs, and I felt peace enwrap me. The sound of seagulls circling above the bay filled the air, adding to the serene atmosphere.

As I stood there, taking in the beauty of the coastal landscape, I felt grateful to have found such a hidden gem to complete my three years of family medicine residency training. The apartment may have been time-worn, but it possessed charm and character that were hard to find in modern buildings. Walking through the apartment brought back memories of being a young boy, running around the military base housing that my sister and I called home for many years. As I left the bedroom, I was certain I had found my sanctuary—a place where I could escape the chaos of the outside world and truly call home.

With my brief tour of the residence now done, I exited the unit to begin hauling in the boxes I could fit inside my sedan. The remainder of my belongings and furniture would arrive later today when the professional movers I had hired delivered everything. As I walked back and forth between the apartment and my vehicle, I stacked the cardboard moving boxes precariously in my arms to minimize the number of times I would need to repeat the process. Moving to a new town—especially one as remote as Frieden Bay—for the next stage of my medical training had been a dream of mine. However, the reality of the process was proving to be more challenging than I had anticipated.

Suddenly, a cheerful voice broke through my thoughts, disrupting the late afternoon silence of the complex.

"Hey there! Can I give you a hand with those boxes?"

Startled, I turned to see a young man with a friendly smile and a thick, black beard standing a few steps away from me. His eyes sparkled with genuine kindness, instantly putting me at ease. Grateful for the offer, I nodded and handed him a couple of the lighter boxes.

"I appreciate the help," I said, relieved to share the burden. "Are you one of the new residents at Alta Vista, too?"

The man chuckled, his voice resonating with warmth and excitement.

"Was it that obvious?" he replied, extending his hand for a handshake. "It's really nice to meet you! I'm Vincent Bronson. I moved to this apartment complex from Orlando about two weeks ago. I recognized you from the roster the program sent out last month."

Surprised by his respectable awareness, I could not help but smile back at him.

"It's great to meet you, too. You said Orlando, right? Did you grow up in Florida?"

"No. I spent most of my early years in the Los Angeles area. I did go to college and medical school down in Orlando, though. In many ways, it feels like my second home."

As we continued carrying the boxes into the apartment, Vincent and I struck up a conversation about our previous experiences and the challenges we each faced during the transition into our new roles. It turned out that Vincent had also moved many times when he was younger, making the jump to Frieden Bay for residency old hat, more or less. We exchanged stories of our hometowns, and he gave me pointers about fun things to do around the area.

Eventually, my curiosity got the best of me.

"What about you, Vincent? Do you have any family or friends here?"

A wistful expression crossed his face, but he quickly shrugged it off, masking it with a smile.

"Unfortunately, no. Everyone's mostly back in California and Mexico. I came here on my own, hoping for a fresh start. It was hard to say goodbye, but I have heard very good things about the training we can get out here."

I nodded, showing solidarity in making such a tough decision.

"But hey, enough about me. What's with all the artwork? I noticed a few interesting pieces in your car."

Looking down at the wrapped frames and other pieces carefully protected for travel, I realized my modest collection of paintings, sculptures, and photographs had become a conversation piece. Creating art was essential to my mother and grandfather; it had always been a way for them to express themselves and connect with others on a deeper level. It reflected their values, passions, and even their past. Over the years, they gave us several pieces that were off-display for a show or sale at a gallery.

Once we got back inside, I gently set down the boxes in my arms and carefully unwrapped one of the oil paintings—a vibrant swirl of colors capturing the essence of a bustling city street with large buildings dotting the skyline. As I explained its importance to me, Vincent attentively listened, his eyes gleaming with curiosity.

"Your mom and grandpa are very skilled artists," he remarked, holding the painting in his hands. "Nobody in my family is an artist, so learning about all of this is fascinating."

Looking at their artwork made me feel homesick and reminded me of how solid of a self-image each of them had as artists. I envied that confidence since I was still figuring out who I was as a physician and person. Within a few more minutes, our combined effort made short work of a long job. After getting everything inside, I invited Vincent into my apartment and set up two canvas chairs for us to sit on while I was still awaiting the arrival of my other items. Many boxes of various sizes surrounded us, all lining the walls to keep the walkways clear.

Sipping on a water bottle he had brought, Vincent glanced at the clutter of boxes. Sheets of sunlight poured through the windows, illuminating each dust mote that danced around us.

"Since I'm already here, would you like me to help you unpack some of these boxes?" he offered, setting his water bottle on the kitchen counter.

I nodded, grateful for his assistance. Pulling at the snug tape of a nearby box, I began distributing some of the closest boxes between us. I pointed out my system for labeling what each box contained. We decided I would work on things for the kitchen while he focused on the living room.

Vincent opened a box labeled 'BOOKS' and pulled out a ragged copy of *Moby-Dick*, other works of fiction, and various textbooks from my school years.

"Planning to build a floor-to-ceiling library?" he teased, his voice echoing slightly in the mostly empty unit.

"I wish," I chuckled, unpacking my minimal kitchen supplies—plates, bowls, silverware, cooking utensils, and a mismatched set of glasses. "I just need to get my mansion first. Also, it might help to have more books, too."

As the afternoon turned into early evening, our silent companionship was filled with the noise of crumpled paper and sliding cardboard. Each object we unpacked seemed like a small victory—a tiny homecoming. I stumbled across an old photo album at the bottom of a particularly stubborn box. Flipping it open, a picture of a much younger me on a bicycle stared back. In another box, I ran my fingers across the spines of my records, crisp as the day they were pressed.

"Oh, now that's the good stuff," he brightened, peering into the same box. "Good old vinyls. I've loved the recent resurgence of these things. It reminds me of summer days with my parents and sisters. Do you have a player?"

"Yeah," I replied, thinking about all the great music I had. "It will come on the moving truck in just a bit."

"We should fire it up as soon as it arrives. You've got everything from Fleetwood Mac to The Smashing Pumpkins in here. These albums take me back."

As I was about to play music from my phone, I received a call from the movers who had my large furniture. I confirmed the unit number and address, and then the mover on the phone mentioned that they would arrive in about thirty minutes to drop off everything and set up the furniture.

"I guess we have time for another box or two before they get here," Vincent concluded, heading over to the opposite side of the room to continue the unpacking.

Vincent found and opened another box labeled 'SCRAPBOOK + OFFICE' and pulled out an old, leather-bound scrapbook I had gotten back when I was ten years old.

"Ah, memories," I announced, taking the scrapbook from Vincent's hands. "I've had this forever."

"Why don't we look through that scrapbook while we're waiting on them?" Vincent suggested. "We could move out to the balcony to enjoy the breeze while we do."

I nodded in silent agreement, grabbing one of the canvas chairs before relocating outside. It had been a long time since I had looked through this scrapbook. It was a mix of memories: some happy and some bittersweet. As Vincent and I settled into our chairs on the otherwise empty balcony, I opened the book and began flipping through the pages. As I flipped to the first page, a rogue wind caught a loose photo of me as a child and started to carry it away. Panicked, I lunged out of my seat and snatched it out of the air, hastily tucking it back into the safety of my scrapbook. Wide-eyed, Vincent and I looked at each other and sighed before returning to the book's contents.

The first few pages were filled with photos from my childhood—birthdays, family vacations, and school events. I grinned at the images of my younger self, remembering the carefree days of my youth. As I turned the page, I came across a photograph of my parents and me standing outside our old home. It was taken the day they dropped me off for my first day of high school. It was a moment frozen in time, a reminder of how much they supported me during my upbringing.

Vincent peered over my shoulder at the book, his arm resting casually on the back of my chair. I sincerely appreciated how invested he was in getting to know more about me, especially since we were strangers just a few hours ago. He understood this moment's significance: going through my memories and revisiting the past.

I continued to flip through the pages, reliving moments of laughter and joy, heartbreak and loss. There were photos of old friends, past relationships, and places I had visited. Certificates from my primary and secondary school years filled over a dozen pages, serving as powerful reminders of my achievements. Each page told a story, a chapter in my life that had shaped me into the person I had become.

As we reached the end of the scrapbook, a lump formed in my throat. I had not realized how much emotion would come flooding back to me as I replayed these memories in my mind. Vincent patted my back, clearly sensing that this was an emotional experience.

"I'm so impressed by how well you and your family were able to document things over time," he said gently. "I learned so much about you from just looking at the photos and other things in your scrapbook."

"It has always been a joy to capture the small moments in life," I replied, closing the scrapbook and placing it firmly on my lap. "I want to continue adding to my scrapbook during residency. I don't want to lose track of what's most important to me."

Just then, the doorbell rang, signaling the movers' arrival. Vincent and I got up from our chairs, ready to start this new chapter of our lives in this new place. Now sunset, the apartment looked less like a storage space and more like a home—my new home, witnessed and warmed by a new friend. Vincent took one final sip from his now almost empty water bottle, standing by a west-facing window where the last of the day's light cast a warm glow across his face.

"Looks like you're almost set. Once they bring in your furniture, you'll have a fully functional apartment."

I opened the door to greet the movers and let them inside. We quickly discussed the placement of the main pieces of furniture, including my bed and TV stand. As the movers began unloading the furniture, excitement and anticipation surged inside me like tidal waves.

"Oh, I forgot to mention something to you earlier," Vincent said, smacking his forehead with his palm. "I invited the other interns to have dinner at my apartment this evening. I still need to go to the grocery store and pick up some items for tonight. Would you like to come over and join us?"

After finding out the store was only half a mile away, I grabbed my wallet, and Vincent and I took off after I clarified a few more things for the moving crew. As we strolled through the pleasant town, I took in the beauty of the various houses, municipal buildings, and businesses: all bathed in a golden light at sunset. It was the perfect backdrop for our trip to the grocery store to pick up ingredients for the dinner. Vincent was energetic, chatting about how lucky we were to live and work in such a picturesque place. I concurred with him, except for the suffocating feeling of the three-year commitment I had to shove to the side.

On our walk, Vincent told me what he knew about the other first-year residents. Apparently, we all came from different parts of the country, drawn to this small coastal town for the laid-back charm, tight-knit community, and robust training in primary care. One of the interns came from another country, but Vincent was unsure where exactly. He also disclosed details about the senior residents and our faculty he had discovered online.

As we wandered through the aisles of the grocery store, Vincent excitedly picked out fresh vegetables, meats, and cheeses for the group dinner. Based on the way he spoke about cooking, he had a keen eye for ingredients and a knack for putting together delicious dishes. I could not wait to see what he would come up with for tonight's get-together.

As we made our way back to the apartment complex with our full bags of groceries, Vincent suggested a quick detour to the beach to catch the final moments of sunset. I eagerly agreed, knowing it would be a beautiful sight. We walked along the sandy shore, waves crashing at our feet as the sun dipped lower on the horizon, painting the sky with pink, indigo, and orange hues. As the sun cast a final burst of light across the western sky before disappearing behind the trees and mountains, Vincent clapped his hands together. He announced it was time to head back so he could start preparing the food and welcome the other two interns. As our feet touched the asphalt of the complex's parking lot, we caught sight of two people in the distance.

"I think I see them sitting over there," Vincent declared, gesturing to two young women sitting and speaking with one another on a bench under a lamppost in our apartment complex.

As we approached and greeted them, Vincent introduced me to the other two interns starting with the residency program. There was Soraya Chabahari, a former nurse turned physician in her mid-thirties from Iran. She had a warm smile and a kind demeanor that immediately put me at ease. Soraya had lived in the United States for over twenty years with Ibrahim, her husband, and Mina, her six-year-old daughter. Soraya was passionate about medicine and dedicated to her family, and all of this allowed her to persevere despite the challenges she faced as an immigrant.

Next to Soraya was Beatrice Portinari, a dark-haired and dark-eyed woman of a similar age to me. Beatrice, the daughter of two Italian immigrants, had a more traditional path through college and medical school in the United States. Her quiet confidence and piercing intelligence were immediately apparent. Beatrice spent a significant amount of time in medical school doing public health research, and she indicated how much she wanted to complete a graduate program in public health at some point in her career. She had an air of mystery about her, and I was deeply intrigued by her gravitas.

"I'm so glad we are getting together before we get started on Monday," Vincent stated, smiling at each of us. "Let's head inside and get comfortable. I'll start on dinner right away."

As we sat down to dinner, Vincent broke the ice, and we all began to chat and get to know each other. The conversation flowed easily, and it was clear that we all shared a passion for family medicine and a desire to make a difference in the world. Soraya told stories of her experiences working in underserved communities, while Beatrice spoke about some of her other research in infectious diseases. Their dedication and drive were instantly inspiring to me, but they also made me feel insecure about what I had done with my life thus far.

As the evening went on, we disclosed more about our backgrounds and personal lives. Soraya expanded on the struggles she faced as an immigrant and the challenges of balancing work and family. Beatrice revealed that she had lost her mother to an aggressive form of breast cancer when she was young, and that was what inspired her to pursue a career in medicine. I shared my story of growing up in a small midwestern town and dreaming of becoming a doctor from a young age. With some discomfort, I confessed that substance use disorders ran in my family, which heightened my sensitivity to people dealing with addiction.

As the night came to an end, I felt grateful for the opportunity to work alongside such incredible people: Vincent, with his personality and passion; Soraya, with her resilience and compassion; Beatrice, with her intelligence and determination; and me, with my dreams and aspirations for a productive career in medicine. I knew the next few years of residency would be challenging, but with these three by my side, I felt more confident that we could overcome anything that came our way.

The dinner was a success due to Vincent's fantastic cooking skills and creativity in the kitchen. I saw him beam with pride as we all dug in and enjoyed the feast he had prepared. We toasted to new beginnings and dreams of the future, united by our love for medicine and our interlaced experiences in this beautiful town of Frieden Bay. As we walked out of Vincent's apartment and into the night, we said our goodbyes and made plans to meet again soon.

Despite the pleasantness of the evening, something gnawed at my mind as I lay in bed: I was no longer as deeply connected to the friends and family I had left behind. Although it was incredible to have my co-residents in my life, I could not shake the isolating feeling of being so far away. The unease made me toss and turn for an hour. As I finally drifted off to sleep, I thought I could hear the echo of my voice ridiculing my choices.

CHAPTER THREE

The Beacon

> *Momentary greatness can beget a fool's paradise: a paradise so limitless and so intoxicating that it lulls those who dare bask in its magnificence into a state of moral and intellectual paralysis.*

Inspired by Vincent's enthusiasm for exploration, I woke up early in the morning to walk around the neighborhood where Vincent's and my apartments were located. Frieden Bay had sights strikingly reminiscent of my old college stomping ground, including small family-owned shops and restaurants. With empty cupboards back at my apartment, I headed to a nearby café tucked beneath a monolithic red maple that must have been dozens of years old. Its quaint sign, "The Nook," swayed gently in the cool breeze. As I pushed open the door, the warm, inviting scent of brewed coffee and fresh pastries enveloped me.

Within its four walls, the café was a mosaic of locals; an elderly couple sat by the window, their hands entwined next to steaming cups, while a group of cyclists in the corner animatedly planned their next route. I ordered black coffee and a chocolate croissant before settling down by the fireplace. No sooner had I taken my first sip than the door chime announced another patron. To my surprise, it was Vincent: his face lighting up when he saw me.

"Hey, partner! Small world, eh?" he grinned, pulling up a chair.

"I should say the same to you," I chuckled, gesturing around at the décor of the café. "This place feels like it's from a storybook."

Vincent nodded, looking around appreciatively.

Over breakfast, Vincent regaled me with stories of his travels and explorations around the town—the hidden coves best for sunrise views, the high cliffs ideal for watching storms roll in from the sea, and a tiny bookstore called "The Divine Bookery" that held first editions of classic works on its creaky shelves. He made specific suggestions for places to eat and grab a beer, including a locally famous pub called "The Beacon."

"The Beacon, huh?" I noted, considering how nice it would be to grab a drink at some point today. "I'll probably check that out later."

"It's really cool," Vincent said, talking up the pub. "I would join you, but I have some errands I need to run before orientation on Monday."

With that, Vincent and I parted ways. I headed out of The Nook and went down a cobblestone path toward the center of the town. I passed by multiple fruit stands and ice cream vendors as I scoped out some of Frieden Bay's offerings. From this distance, I could more clearly see the docks and piers, with various ships of wildly different sizes lining the series of wooden walkways. Serendipitously, I encountered the pub Vincent mentioned on the town square's south end.

The doorway leading into The Beacon had a certain majesty that gave me pause. In the light of the noon sun, the gilded portions shone brightly. The bricks forming the pub's exterior seemed to glisten in direct sunlight like twinkling stars against a dusky sky. The pub was inarguably beautiful and sat snugly between two newer-looking businesses: its old-world charm defiant in the face of modern progress.

As I drew closer to the entrance, the aroma of whiskey and beer invited me further. Gently pushing the heavy wooden door open and walking down the stone steps, a tiny bell tinkled above the threshold to welcome me into the establishment. Inside The Beacon, aged books lined the walls, the shelves reached the ceiling, and the dark wooden bar had tales of its own etched into its surface.

"First time at The Beacon?" a man behind the bar asked loudly, revealing a knowing smirk as he cleaned a wine glass.

"Yes," I admitted. "Something about this place caught my eye, and a friend spoke highly of it."

"That's the magic of The Beacon," the man said as he set the glass down. "This pub has been in my family for five generations. It's always been a place of new beginnings—a place where new relationships bloom. Each corner of this place hides stories; if you're lucky, you might discover one yourself."

Curiosity piqued, I took a seat at the bar and ordered a pint of local Indian pale ale, which the bartender served with a flourish.

"You see that doorway when you came in?" he inquired, leaning toward me across the bar. "Legend has it that it's not just an ordinary doorway. They say it's a gateway, a doorway to anywhere. My grandfather told me that once a year, during the summer solstice, it opens to a different time and place."

Skepticism must have shown on my face because the bartender chortled.

"Not one for legends, huh? Well, I was like you until one summer night when curiosity got the best of me. I stayed past midnight, and that's when it happened."

"What happened?" I asked, my incredulity fading.

"The doorway glowed with a soft, golden light, and through it, I could see a street that wasn't of our time. People in Victorian garb walked past, oblivious to my presence," he recounted, his eyes lost in the memory.

A deep laugh could be heard from another patron a few seats down from me at the bar.

"Tom, are you telling your 'stories' to another newbie again?" the person said, shaking his head in Tom's direction.

"It's real, I tell you, Virgil," Tom insisted, exasperated by the question. "Well, whatever. I hope you enjoy your visit here today."

With that, the bartender retreated to the corner, where he busied himself with organizing liquor bottles.

"Sorry about my friend over there," the stranger named Virgil said as he stretched his arms above his head. "He's a bit eccentric but a good guy all the same."

"No worries," I said, sipping my IPA. "It was definitely entertaining. He had me going, for sure."

"Virgil Altamura," he insouciantly reported as he extended his hand to shake mine. "It is a pleasure to meet you."

"Likewise," I responded, popping down from the stool to shake his hand. "Say, your name and face seem very familiar to me, but I cannot put my finger on why."

Virgil examined my face closely for a few seconds before snapping his fingers and smiling.

"You're one of the new interns, right?" he asked, confident in his guess.

"That's right. I'm excited about getting started with the program. I take it you are with the program, too. Oh, wait…"

I paused for a moment to gather my thoughts. *Where did I see his name and face before?* Then, I had an epiphany.

"I remember seeing your name now; it was on the roster. You're Dr. Altamura."

"Yes, I'm one of the Alta Vista Family Medicine Residency faculty members."

"What can you tell me about our training program?" I ventured, taking a new seat closer to Dr. Altamura.

Dr. Altamura leaned back in his chair, studying me momentarily before responding.

"Our training program is one of the best in the nation for primary care," he said, a self-assured smile on his lips. "We have a rigorous curriculum designed to challenge you in ways that will safely push you beyond your limits. With the right amount of effort and commitment to the curriculum, you will become an exceptional family doc. You'll be ready to go into any community and serve the people there."

I nodded, feeling nervousness and exhilaration emerging at his words. Becoming a family physician was my dream from medical school, and matching at this residency program was the culmination of years of hard work and dedication.

"You will be tested every step of the way."

He paused. His brow wrinkled. After a few seconds of silence, Dr. Altamura took a sip and continued.

"Our program is known for its high standards and sometimes demanding rotations. You will be expected to work long hours, handle a heavy workload, and make difficult decisions under pressure. Are you prepared for that?"

I swallowed, steeling myself for the challenge ahead.

"I am prepared, Dr. Altamura. I'm ready to give it my all."

He nodded at me, signaling his satisfaction with my response.

"Good," he said. "We need physicians who are knowledgeable, resilient, compassionate, and dedicated. This path requires sacrifice, but it's also immensely rewarding. You have the opportunity to improve and save lives, to make a difference in the world. Remember that, especially on the tough days."

Dr. Altamura bowed his head for a moment as if in a deep reverie. I took the momentary gap in our conversation to finish my ale and place my pint glass down farther on the bar for pickup. As he raised his head, I noticed a more relaxed smile, suggesting an imminent change in conversation.

"So, what do you do outside of work to keep yourself balanced?" he inquired, leaning back in his seat.

"I have always been invested in writing," I replied, staring down at the wooden countertop. "Ever since college, I've had to relegate it to the bottom of my priority list so I could focus on coursework and progressing through my medical training."

"That resonates with me," he said, a wry grin overtaking his face. "I had to give up painting for far too long. It was my lovely wife Patricia who got me back into sharpening the saw of my craft."

"It's so tough in this line of work," I said. "You mentioned making sacrifices, and I feel that one thing we often sacrifice but don't talk enough about is what makes us whole. Hobbies, passions, pastimes. I have been grappling with that issue for a while."

Dr. Altamura nodded in understanding, taking a sip of his ale as he listened intently. I appreciated his genuine interest in my passions outside of work. The conversation reminded me of meeting Vincent. It was a refreshing change from my usual clinically oriented conversations with fellow healthcare professionals.

"I'd like to know more. What do you enjoy writing about?" he asked curiously.

"I mainly write analytical and persuasive pieces—essays, op-eds, and perspective articles," I explained. "But, my heart lies in the world of fiction. I love creating new worlds and characters and exploring different themes and emotions through my stories. I am deeply invested in exploring people's relationships and what those relationships reveal about humanity and the human experience."

"That's wonderful," Dr. Altamura said, his tone encouraging. "Writing can be a great outlet for self-expression and externalizing our internal worlds. Do you have any particular projects you're currently working on?"

I hesitated, unsure whether I should speak openly with him about my writing. It was a deeply personal story that delved into my struggles and life experiences. However, something about Dr. Altamura's presence reassured me and made me trust him with my innermost feelings.

"I've been working on a novel for a long time," I confessed sheepishly. "It's gone through many iterations. It's about an artist striving for perfection in an imperfect world. It is an ironic story about what it means to create art and how art is inherently imperfect. Ultimately, the artist destroys himself in the pursuit of artistic perfection. In some ways, it is an allegory for modern life, especially in a field like ours."

Dr. Altamura's expression softened, a look of empathy in his eyes.

"That sounds like a powerful story," he remarked. "That reminds me a lot of Franz Kafka's work. It takes courage to confront such a complicated subject like that. I appreciate your willingness to share that part of yourself with others."

After revealing that to Dr. Altamura, I felt a weight lift off my shoulders. It was rare to find someone who truly understood the therapeutic and transcendent value of writing, someone who did not dismiss it as just a silly hobby. Dr. Altamura's support and validation meant more to me than he could ever know. As our conversation continued, we discussed deeper topics, discussing the importance of self-care and balance in our frequently tumultuous lives. Dr. Altamura described his struggles with maintaining work-life balance, admitting that he often found solace in painting sessions with his wife.

Time flew by as we sat in the pub talking about life. Dr. Altamura spoke of his journey in medicine, recounting the trials and tribulations he had faced, the personal obstacles he had overcome, and how he had emerged stronger. He recounted anecdotes from his early days as a resident, his eyes gleaming with nostalgia and a tinge of melancholy.

"You know, being a family doc is not just a profession. It becomes a part of who you are," he said, his voice heavy with emotion. "There's a deep sense of responsibility that comes with this job. To be there for your patients, to support them in their darkest moments, to make decisions that could mean life or death—it's a tremendous burden to bear. But it is also an incredible honor and privilege."

At that moment, I was reminded that being a physician was not just about acquiring knowledge and honing skills—it was about embodying compassion, empathy, and a genuine desire to help others. It was about being present with other people. It was about recognizing the power of human connection, of being there for those in need. Those values were the very same that drew me into pursuing family medicine as my specialty.

"Would you like to visit an overlook here in town?" Dr. Altamura's face brightened. "I get a lot of peace and inspiration from being up there. Several references I have used for my paintings came from pictures I took up there."

"That sounds great," I agreed, finishing off another ale.

With that, we moseyed out of the cool pub into the sultry air of the late afternoon. We walked along the paved streets up to a trailhead on the other side of town. Located on the outskirts of Frieden Bay, the overlook was a well-kept secret. Dr. Altamura told me he had stumbled upon it three years ago while exploring the town, and it quickly became his favorite spot to relax, meditate, and get ideas for new paintings. As we hiked up the steep trail, I took in the spectacular views of the town below and the shimmering bay in the distance.

As we reached the top, I was greeted by a panoramic view of Frieden Bay spread out before me. The sun was low in the sky, starting to cast a golden glow over the town and creating a magical atmosphere. I could see the sprawling docks, the quaint houses that looked like little dots, and the lush greenery surrounding the area. Dr. Altamura led me to a large rock overlooking the town where we could relax. We sat for several minutes, mindful of our environment's beauty. The gentle wind rustled through the trees, carrying the scent of pine I remembered from my arrival. I closed my eyes and took a deep breath, feeling at peace. For a moment, I was back on my balcony with Vincent, ruffling through memories and breathing in the same sea breeze as it climbed to reach us.

From this vantage point, the town looked so peaceful and serene; I could understand why Dr. Altamura found solace in this place. As the sky darkened, we sat in companionable silence for a while, watching the town below slowly light up as the streetlights came to life. Dr. Altamura turned to me with a smile as the stars twinkled in the night sky. I smiled back, grateful to experience such beauty and tranquility. Frieden Bay had captured my heart in more ways than one, and I knew that this overlook would hold a special place in my memories. As we made our way back down the trail, the muffled sounds of the town powering down for the night graced my ears. Dr. Altamura showed me a side of my new home that I had not yet seen, and that gesture deserved my utmost gratitude.

As we reached the bottom of the trail, I looked at the overlook one last time and then took my leave to head back to my apartment. When I turned back around to trek home, the fear of being trapped reared its head again, much like it did when I sat in Mr. Haron's office. *What if I hate this program and despise living in Frieden Bay?* Just then, I thought I saw a dark presence out of the corner of my eye. However, I found nothing when I whirled around to inspect my surroundings. It was odd, but surely it was just the poor lighting of the night playing tricks on me.

CHAPTER FOUR

Perspectives

> *Once one steps into the false paradise, one enters into the permanent chrysalis of one's life's achievement, never to emerge as a transformed and better form of the original self.*

The faint buzzing of my phone against my oak bureau stirred me from my slumber ahead of the scheduled alarm. I groggily sat up and reached out to grab the vibrating device; Vincent had sent me three text messages.

"Pastry or coffee from Greta's?" the messages collectively read, with the final message containing just the question mark.

How nice of him to offer, I thought, typing out my response to request a hazelnut latte and chocolate croissant.

"Cool! I'll bring those to the hospital," his response message read.

With that, I quickly showered and dressed in proper business attire for the first day of orientation for the residency program. I knew my fellow interns and Dr. Altamura so far, and the prospect of meeting the rest of the residents and faculty was fascinating as much as it was anxiety-provoking. Everyone had been so kind and gregarious, which made moving from a distant place much easier than it would have been otherwise. However, I needed to get more information about my environment before I would feel entirely comfortable in it.

I glanced at my map app to triple-check the location of Alta Vista Hospital, where I would spend a large part of the next three years. It was a smaller community hospital, serving somewhere in the ballpark of fifteen thousand patients in Frieden Bay and the catchment area. It had somewhere north of one hundred beds to provide inpatient services to people needing that level of care. On the map, I also noted the location of Alta Vista Primary Care Center, which was just across the street from the hospital. This clinic was where the residents would provide outpatient care to people in our community and establish continuity of care.

I gave myself extra lead time to make sure that I had the opportunity to scope out the area thoroughly and understand the route I would be taking to get over to the hospital and clinic. It was an unexpectedly scenic route, taking me across a stone bridge overlooking the main part of the town as it sloped down toward the coastline. The final winding road led downhill to a valley where the hospital stood like a titan among the trees and stones. A small cooperative market stood nestled into one of the smaller mountains, representing a place I would likely become very familiar with in my day-to-day routine.

On entering the hospital, I noted the vaulted ceilings of the lobby, the bright colors of the scattered signage and LED displays, and the gorgeous artwork lining the walls of the first floor. An older woman wearing a purple vest and name tag with the word "Volunteer" on it sat behind a brightly colored desk several feet in front of the entrance. Her warm smile and gentle disposition made for a welcoming first impression at this facility. She politely asked if I needed help finding where I needed to go and pointed the way to the conference room where I would meet with the others in our program.

I followed a long corridor to the other side of the first floor, which was lined with large windows allowing a lot of natural light into the space. The light from the sun drew attention to the numerous framed headshots of the physicians and other healthcare providers working at Alta Vista. On glass-encased bulletin boards just a few steps down from the lines of framed photographs, I found the roster pictures of all of the residents at the hospital, which included family medicine, internal medicine, pediatrics, and general surgery. The intricately designed program logo containing imagery of the sea, mountains, and forests adorned the top of our roster sheet. Next to this was a roster of the program faculty and staff, mainly featuring unfamiliar pictures of everyone from the Program Director to the Program Manager.

As I entered the main conference room, I looked at the other three first-year resident physicians who had arrived before me. Vincent, Soraya, and Beatrice waved at me from their table close to the front of the room and beckoned me over to join them. On my way over, I briefly introduced myself to two faculty members. They warmly welcomed me to the program and expressed their eagerness to get to know us better later in the day. At the front of the room, near a large screen showing the program name and logo, I saw Dr. Altamura energetically chatting with a redheaded, bespectacled woman who must be another of the faculty members.

Almost immediately after I nervously lowered myself into a chair between Vincent and Beatrice, a jovial, middle-aged man with a large, flowing mustache made his way to the podium next to the screen. His face looked very familiar, and I soon realized he was one of my interviewers from months back.

"Good morning, everybody!" he projected his voice across the room. "We have a small but mighty group of new interns here today. It has been a while since I last spoke with you during your interviews. To reintroduce myself, I am Dr. Alexander Calisto, your Program Director for the Alta Vista Family Medicine Residency Program."

"This guy is a phenom in our specialty," Vincent leaned in and whispered to me. "You should check out his CV after orientation today. You will not be disappointed."

Dr. Calisto began the introductory presentation by describing his experiences as a resident and the lessons he learned during his medical training. He emphasized the importance of teamwork and support within the program, assuring us that this would be a transformative experience that would shape us into skilled and compassionate family physicians. His words offered reassurance, and my nerves slowly dissipated the longer he spoke.

"Now, I would like to introduce you to the other faculty who will be teaching and mentoring you over the next three years," Dr. Calisto stated, gesturing toward the other attending physicians in the room. "To my right sits Dr. Richard Coffman, your Associate Program Director. To my left sit Drs. Virgil Altamura and Michelle Mose, your Family Medicine Core Faculty."

The four of us clapped to show our appreciation for having them with us for today's orientation.

"We are committed to providing you with the education you need to go out and care for your communities as family physicians," Dr. Calisto said. "Now, let's do some icebreakers as a group."

With the formal introductions out of the way, Dr. Calisto brought everyone together around a single table and encouraged us to mingle so we could get to know one another. Initially, we exchanged pleasantries and shared our current and past aspirations for becoming family physicians. We played two truths and a lie for our first icebreaker activity, which proved far more enlightening and hilarious than I expected. We learned that Dr. Mose grew up in British Columbia, Canada, that Dr. Altamura was an avid seafarer, and that Dr. Calisto once had nine unpaid parking tickets at the same time while in college. As I listened to my peers' stories and aspirations once again, I realized that I was among a group of individuals bound not only by a professional identity but also by a deep desire to make a positive impact.

At noon, the residents in their second and third years joined us for a group lunch, during which we met the entire resident complement in one place. Isaiah Kirkpatrick, the current Chief Resident, came over first to welcome us and offer us his support should we need anything at any point. Slowly but surely, we made the rounds to meet the other eight residents in the program, and the diversity of their cohorts was as rich and substantial as our own. We socialized so much that I completely neglected to eat lunch.

Throughout the one-week orientation, we engaged in various team-building activities and workshops, ranging from the human-knot game to clinical skills sessions for suturing and long-acting reversible contraception placement. Dr. Calisto introduced us to the hospital staff, familiarized us with the hospital's electronic health record system, and guided us through the intricate processes of being a resident physician. He encouraged us to ask questions, seek help when needed, and reminded us that we would never be alone in this journey. He emphasized that all of the faculty and senior residents were there to support our progression through graduate medical education. With every word of reassurance, my initial nervousness faded and gave way to cautious optimism.

On Thursday at lunchtime, my co-interns and I decided to have a meal together at a new ramen bar that opened on the north side of the town square. As our group approached the restaurant, we noticed the restaurant stood impressively tall for the area, boasting an elegant Japanese-style pagoda design inviting all onlookers inside. Entering the building, the snug interior and aromatic potted plants instantly impressed us. A polite host greeted us before taking us back to our table, neatly set up for traditional dining.

"I feel so spoiled because of everything they've been doing for us," I confessed, gradually settling into a cross-legged position on the floor mat. "Dr. Calisto and the others have been great. I can't lie: I was worried we would end up with a rough crowd based on what other residents said online."

"I felt the same way," Vincent concurred, awkwardly positioning himself on his knees. "I knew we would be in good hands as soon as I started reading up on our faculty. They make me feel like I've done nothing with my life so far! Ugh, it hurts to sit this way, but at least the food will be amazing."

"I haven't had a good bowl of ramen in years," Soraya thought aloud, rubbing her face. "No better way to break the dry spell than with good company."

"Didn't Dr. Calisto say he would pay us back for lunch?" Beatrice inquired, beginning to peruse the extensive lunch menu. "He's such a big teddy bear. I love his energy."

Over lunch, the conversations flowed effortlessly as we exchanged tales of our pre-medicine lives and laughed at Vincent's irreverent jokes. The four of us learned even more about each other—the dreams, struggles, and choices that had brought us to this point in our lives. It felt as if we had known each other for years, connected by a similar passion and a deep understanding of the challenges we faced as new physicians in a new community.

Beatrice told us she was born and raised in a small town on the East Coast, not too dissimilar from Frieden Bay. We bonded over leaving our hometowns to pursue our goals of becoming family physicians. As our conversation continued, I learned that Beatrice was passionate about community health and wellness. She hoped she would eventually work in underserved areas, providing healthcare to those who would otherwise struggle to access it. Her conviction inspired me to think about how I could make a difference in my own career.

Vincent then joined in, talking about his upbringing. Originally from Mexico, he loved adventure and bicycling, and he regaled us with fascinating stories of his travels across his home country. As Vincent spoke, his eyes lit up elatedly, and his hands gestured wildly, transporting us into the heart of Mexico. He spoke of the rugged terrains, the stunning landscapes, and the vibrant culture he had experienced on his biking expeditions. It was as if he carried a piece of his home within him, and his stories were a reminder of the beauty that awaited us beyond the confines of the hospital.

As Soraya took her turn, the tone of the conversation shifted from the adventurous to the introspective. Originally from Tehran, she vividly described the layered complexities of growing up in a family deeply rooted in the arts. Her life was a canvas painted with the broad strokes of classical Persian poetry and the delicate details of traditional music. She argued that medicine is just another art form, musing thoughtfully with her voice as melodic as the music she grew up with. She noted how Frieden Bay attracts artists from all over the world and how we should take full advantage of the opportunity to support artists and enrich our education. We nodded in agreement, moved by her poetic perspective on our chosen field.

When it was my turn, I entertained my companions with funny stories about growing up with a sister who would frequently roughhouse with me and two young parents who were figuring out life at the same time we were. I described growing up as a military brat, traveling the world from the age of five until I was in fourth grade. I detailed my professional plans to open an outpatient clinic similar to one that operated in my hometown: one half dedicated to being a continuity clinic and the other to acute care for established clinic patients. I also talked about my public health work abroad, especially the weeks I spent building wells, a school, and a pharmacy in Honduras.

After we had eaten our fill of the most scrumptious ramen we had ever had, we departed as a group, eager to explore our quaint town. With the afternoon off to do as we pleased, we found ourselves drawn to the local market, where the four of us sampled delicious treats and indulged in some retail therapy. As we wandered through the well-maintained streets, we stumbled upon a small, privately owned clinic: a reminder of why we had come together in the first place. We peered through the windows and imagined what it would be like to practice medicine in a place like that.

Closer to The Beacon and south of the square, we came across an open-air art market, which hosted different kinds of artists from many places. Tapestries, embroideries, sculptures, and landscapes one could view from the sidewalk all focused on distinct subjects like a ship departing from a port or a child reaching up toward his mother. We browsed the works for sale under the tents set up all across the lot. With the little money I had set aside for miscellaneous expenses, I bought a couple of beautiful prints from a young Choctaw artist, which I would frame over the weekend.

The sun began to set, casting a warm-colored glow across the town. We returned to the main path that led to our places of residence, feeling grateful for the connections we had made, the similar dreams, and the beautiful moments we had today. We discussed that we would carpool tomorrow since we were all scheduled to meet outside of the town proper. With each passing day, I slept more easily that night, feeling increasingly optimistic about the next three years.

THE NEXT MORNING, WE GATHERED IN THE WOODS A FEW miles northeast of the hospital to participate in team-building activities. The daylight was strong, and a light breeze rustled the leaves in the trees, creating a relaxing atmosphere. Every resident and faculty member convened at the campgrounds nearest Lion's Mane Falls, and we were all thrilled to join in on this tradition within the program. As soon as the announcement was made that we needed to do so, Vincent and I paired up. We had bonded over the past few days at the hospital, and I felt closer to him than anyone else. In many ways, he felt like my long-lost brother. As our master of ceremony, Dr. Calisto took his place in the middle of the group, informing us of the schedule for activities today. He noted that the residents would stay together for the first portion before splitting up by year for small-group team-building exercises.

As we walked toward the low-ropes course, I could feel the excitement building in my chest. I had always loved adventure and challenges and knew this would be a great experience. The low-ropes course was a series of obstacles suspended just a few feet off the ground. We were supposed to navigate them by leaning on each other for support. Fortunately, Vincent and I had the chance to observe several other pairs go first—including Soraya and Beatrice as a dynamic duo—before setting foot on the ropes ourselves. From afar, we energetically whispered about strategies, making mental notes about what would and would not work for us.

When our time came, Vincent and I stood at the starting point, sizing up the first obstacle before us. We had to walk across a narrow plank while holding onto each other's shoulders for balance. I took a deep breath and stepped onto the plank, feeling it wobble slightly under my weight. Vincent followed closely behind me, his grip firm on my shoulders. As we moved forward, I could feel his solid and reassuring presence. We made it to the other side without any mishaps, and I let out a sigh of relief.

The next obstacle was a series of ropes we had to swing across, using each other's weight to propel ourselves forward. It was a daunting task, and I felt a rush of apprehension sweep through my chest. I hoped I could trust Vincent completely. We swung from rope to rope, cheering each other on through the background of supportive clapping from our co-residents. When we reached the other side, we high-fived each other in triumph. As we progressed through the course, I felt a bond forming between us beyond just partnership.

Finally, we reached the last obstacle of the course: a V-shaped pair of ropes that widened the farther along you went.

No other pairs cleared this obstacle, which put much pressure on us to overcome this last one. Placing our hands together, we inched out onto our respective ropes, leaning forward to maintain our balance as we did. Deciding that we did not have enough of a challenge with this final stretch, Vincent told jokes to the group, explicitly trying to get me to laugh.

"You know, you have the most beautiful eyes," he said as we were stretched out on each side of the gap.

"You, too, Vin," I played along, huffing with the fatigue of holding my weight against Vincent's hands.

The rest of the group cheered as we crossed to the end of the obstacle and stepped victoriously up on the final platform. Our co-residents and faculty slapped us on the back and congratulated us on a job well done as we hunched over, both winded from the last section of the course. Sweaty and exhilarated, Vincent and I grinned at each other, our faces flushed with pride. From there, we divided into year-specific cohorts, doing hilarious team-building activities involving leapfrog, hula-hoops, and medicine balls. By the end of the day, we were exhausted but content, all having enjoyed the time to bond and strengthen our relationships. On the drive home, I treated my colleagues to some root beer floats at a local fast-food restaurant, commemorating the final day of our orientation.

That day in the woods was a turning point for me. While I recognized I could lean on my colleagues when I needed support, I was under no illusions: we would all have our own specific trials and tribulations. I would need to navigate some of these on my own. Some of my hardships would be difficult to articulate to those who care about me. The thought of the challenges ahead made me more anxious about work on Monday. But first, we had plans with Dr. Altamura.

CHAPTER FIVE

Nautical Penchants

The fool becomes a static and incorrigible author of a book only it yearns to read, and as the fool does so, it considers itself a mighty king of infinite space within a nutshell. The idea alone is harrowing enough and serves as a cruel parable condemning an immoral pursuit of singularity.

Running behind schedule, I nervously ran down a path leading to the docks to meet up with Dr. Altamura, who had offered to take the new interns out on an annual boat tour of the bay and farther-reaching Frieden Sea. He mentioned that this was his favorite tradition every year because it effectively instilled in the interns how imperative it is to keep life in perspective during family medicine training. I also secretly thought it was because he knew how impressive it was to operate a boat and freely explore the sea.

As I arrived at the dock, the sun glistened over the calm waters, casting an almost white hue that seemed to promise an idyllic day ahead. I made it just in time to see Dr. Altamura standing at the edge of the dock, a big smile on his face. Next to his head were the words *The Albatross* painted in giant letters across the side of the vessel. Dr. Altamura's boat was quaint but sturdy, a reflection of his personality. It was clear that he had put a lot of love and care into maintaining it.

He greeted me warmly and gestured for me to hurry aboard the boat. I thanked him for inviting me to participate in this outing, and he simply nodded before starting the engine and taking us out onto the open waters. As we set off, I marveled at the vast expanse of the sea stretching out before us. The waves gently rocked our boat, creating a soothing rhythm that eased any tension from my shoulders. We settled on the deck at the bow, our legs dangling lazily over the side as we watched the world around us expand in all directions.

Once we were settled, Dr. Altamura gave us a quick tour of his vessel, proudly pointing out every nook and cranny. *The Albatross* had seen many adventures, and Dr. Altamura had countless stories about it. But today, our adventure was simply to be at sea, away from the shore and the worries of daily life. Eventually, Dr. Altamura suggested we check out the kitchenette in the main cabin for drinks while he kept an eye on the waters.

As we cruised over the choppy waves, Dr. Altamura began talking about the importance of balancing work and personal life, a topic he had touched on before when we were sipping IPAs at The Beacon before orientation. He told us about his own experience as a family physician, emphasizing the need for self-care and time with loved ones. He even revealed some regrets from the early days of his career, adding depth to what I already knew about him. The interns listened intently, absorbing every word he spoke. I reflected on Dr. Altamura's wisdom and his genuine care for his learners.

After a while, Dr. Altamura turned off the engine and let the boat drift in the calm waters many miles away from the town. Being out on the open waters made me feel like an infinitesimal speck of dirt on a great mountain. He encouraged us to take a moment to appreciate the splendor of our surroundings and feel comfortable in not trying to control the immeasurable vastness of the Frieden Sea, likening it to the modern practice of medicine. We sat in silence, each lost in our thoughts.

"Alright, team," Dr. Altamura broke the silence with his deep voice. "Let's come and sit in a circle on the deck. I want us to have some guided discussions about the crazy lives we lead."

We all obeyed, forming what we could of a circle given our small group size. Dr. Altamura disappeared into his cabin for a few minutes only to reappear with a sizable yellow notepad and a pen.

"For our first prompt," he started, his head lowered as he jotted down a few notes. "I want you all to take about two minutes to think about this question: 'What does perfection look like?'"

I tipped my head in mute contemplation, envisioning what I associated with perfection. In my mind, I saw myself standing with my long white coat on, standing on a hill above a crowd of patients shouting my name and cheering for me. I also saw my long-anticipated novel in my hands, a symbol of my success as a writer. I also pictured a big house and a comically large bag of money beside it.

"Okay," he then said after the time had elapsed. "Who would like to share what they saw in their head when they thought about perfection?"

"I had this image of me as a well-respected and beloved physician with wealth and power," Vincent volunteered, seemingly forming a telepathic connection with me. "Finally being done with training and having all the skills I need to do my work excellently."

Beatrice and Soraya nodded enthusiastically in agreement. I joined in to communicate that I also thought up what Vincent eloquently conveyed.

"I love this exercise because I tend to take a different stance on the subject," Dr. Altamura mildly stated, rolling up the sleeves of his crisp maroon dress shirt. "Perfection does exist because there are those among us who believe in its existence. Perfection is subjective; nature has no room for the static form perfection brings. Though it exists to those who choose to see it, it is limited by how we frame it. Art and science are not so dissimilar in this sense: both strive to represent the natural and unnatural within the confines of a frame. So, perfection exists in the finite."

Vincent and I made eye contact and grinned in amusement; we had no idea Dr. Altamura was secretly Aristotle in disguise.

"Perfection is limited to the layer on which it's perceived," he continued to expound. "Beneath it, who knows? Perhaps a seemingly perfect, undisturbed sea is underpinned by offensive and clashing lines, like currents colliding recklessly. We don't know what we don't know in most cases. Truth as we know it is nothing but several smaller truths approximating it. The only thing that is certain about perfection is that having pleasure in what we do gets us as close to perfection as we could hope to be."

"Very true," Vincent declared, his eyes wide. "Did you ever struggle with the pitfalls of perfectionism when you were younger? Or impostor syndrome?"

"That's a great question," Dr. Altamura responded. "Let me show you all something to answer that."

Dr. Altamura reached into a small compartment near the cabin and pulled out an old scrapbook. Its pages were yellowed and worn, telling tales of his medical training and accomplishments throughout his career. I had to restrain myself because I was so excited when I saw his scrapbook. As he turned each page, memories came flooding back to him, and he began to open up about the struggles he faced as a young physician.

"I remember the day like it was yesterday," Dr. Altamura began, his voice shaking slightly. "It was my second week as a freshly minted attending. I had taken a job as a hospitalist at a safety-net hospital in rural Pennsylvania, where I was the only physician for a twenty-bed medical unit. One evening, while on call, an elderly man was admitted for a stroke. The initial imaging of his head showed no blood, so we proceeded with aspirin and careful blood pressure control as usual. Then, out of the blue, I received a call that he had developed new deficits."

He paused for a few seconds, measuring his words and managing his emotions.

"His blood pressure got too low, and he started losing brain tissue beyond his clot. On top of that, he developed a spontaneous brain bleed—the dreaded hemorrhagic conversion. I was too slow to recognize it and to order his repeat head imaging. Once I realized my error, it was too late. We did everything we could, but he couldn't hold on. It was heartbreaking to see him slip away right in front of our eyes."

The group fell silent; each person was lost in their reflections. Only the sounds of the wind and waves disturbed the silence. After about a minute, Dr. Altamura continued with slow and measured words.

"After he passed, I was consumed with shame and self-doubt. I kept thinking, 'What could I have done differently? Why hadn't I been better? Could I have saved him if I had acted faster? Did I deserve to be a physician?' It was a heavy burden to carry, one that weighed me down for years."

My colleagues and I nodded in understanding, our faces mirroring the pain in Dr. Altamura's eyes. We had all been there in our own ways; we had all lost patients or loved ones about whom we cared deeply. It was a part of the job that never got easier, no matter how often we faced it.

"I couldn't sleep, couldn't eat," Dr. Altamura continued. "I felt like I was drowning in grief, suffocating under the weight of my emotions. It was my wife who helped me through those dark days, who held me close and reminded me that I was only human and that I couldn't save everyone. She affirmed my worth as a doctor, husband, and person."

His voice broke, tears gathering in his eyes. Each of us reached out to him, offering silent support. We recognized how hard it was to open up about these things, to show vulnerability in a profession that demanded strength and resilience. Seeing someone in a leadership position be vulnerable was particularly moving.

"It was through my relationships with others—my colleagues, my wife, my friends—that I was able to navigate the trauma of losing that patient," Dr. Altamura said, his voice steadier now. "Talking about it, opening up about my feelings, seeking comfort in the arms of those who cared about me—that's what got me through the dark times."

The circle was quiet; the only sound was soft sniffles. Dr. Altamura looked around at us, grateful for our presence and attention.

"We're not alone in this," he said, his voice filled with conviction. "We have each other, we have our loved ones. We can weather any storm together, no matter how violent."

As his words hung around us, the circle filled with solidarity and unity in the face of grief and loss. Dr. Altamura said he knew that he would never forget the patient he had lost, but he also acknowledged that the loss did not define him. Instead, his personhood was defined by the relationships he cultivated and the love and support he had given and received. With that knowledge, he stood up with elevated spirits and a readiness to dive into further discussions with the group.

Before continuing, Dr. Altamura brought several chilled cans of flavored seltzer water and placed them in the center of our makeshift circle. The condensation on each glistened in the sun's light, reflecting the visages of everyone sitting there. Vincent, Beatrice, Soraya, and I exchanged nervous glances, unsure where this discussion would take us next. At the same time, I looked at each of my colleagues and felt a weird discomfort rise like scalding steam into my throat. *Why did I feel this way?* Part of me felt like a fish out of water—flopping around like an impostor.

After clearing his throat, Dr. Altamura began with a soft yet commanding voice.

"What's your greatest fear as you start your medical career?"

The question hung in the air like a heavy cloud, casting a shadow over our hopes and goals for our professional development.

Vincent spoke up first. His voice trembled as he confessed, "I fear making a mistake that could cost someone's life. Holding someone's life in my hands is overwhelming, and I worry that I may not be capable enough to handle it."

Dr. Altamura wordlessly communicated his understanding.

"It's a common fear among medical professionals, Vincent," he remarked. "Remember: mistakes are a part of the learning process. What matters is how you handle them and use them to become incrementally better."

Next, Beatrice, a person who would likely have an outsized impact on our specialty, divulged her fear.

"I'm terrified of becoming desensitized to the pain and suffering of my patients. It's easy to become disconnected in this field when you burn out, and I worry that I may lose touch with my humanity in the pursuit of treating and preventing disease."

Dr. Altamura placed a hand on Beatrice's shoulder, offering her reassurance.

"It's important to remember the humanity of your patients, Beatrice. Compassion and communication are just as crucial as medical knowledge in this profession. The easiest way to avoid the pitfall you described is to nurture the garden of your relationships every day and seek support when you need it."

Soraya took a deep breath before speaking.

"My greatest fear is being unable to provide the care and support my patients need. I often worry that I won't be able to make a difference in their lives, no matter how hard I try. I am also scared of not being able to balance my work with taking care of my family."

Dr. Altamura smiled warmly at Soraya, his eyes brimming with pride.

"Your dedication and compassion will guide you, Soraya. Trust in yourself and your abilities, and you will make a difference in the lives of your patients. Just remember that change can be slow, and sometimes, we have to be patient to see it."

Finally, it was my turn to speak. I hesitated for a moment, unsure how to express my fear. It was peculiar because I had articulated this so easily to Dr. Altamura several days ago. To center myself, I drew in a deep breath and held it for a few seconds before speaking.

"I'm scared of losing myself in the demanding nature of this profession. I fear that I'll sacrifice my own well-being and happiness in the pursuit of excellence, neglecting the things that truly matter in life."

Dr. Altamura's gaze softened as he looked at me, a sense of understanding passing between us.

"Balance is key in our work. Take care of yourself so that you can take care of others. Your well-being is just as important as your patients'. Keep this in mind: smelling the roses only takes a moment."

We then dove into discussions about the sacrifices of being a healer, the days that bleed into each other, and the toll it takes on one's well-being. But amidst all the challenges, Dr. Altamura's voice had an undeniable sense of purpose. He spoke of the gratitude he felt for being able to make a difference and bring comfort and hope to those in need.

"What do you not want to lose in pursuing a career in family medicine?" Dr. Altamura asked as we transitioned to a profoundly reflective part of our conversation.

It was a question that seemed simple, yet it was fraught with as much complexity as the decision to enter medicine itself. I watched as Vincent—always ready—responded, his voice steady and thoughtful.

"For me, it's my understanding and connection with nature. Medicine is a field grounded in science, sure, but it's also an art that mimics the natural world in many ways. I'm concerned that, in the busy corridors of the hospital and clinic, I may forget the serenity found in the simple wonders of nature that once inspired me to become a physician."

Dr. Altamura nodded lightly and encouragingly.

Then Soraya leaned forward. Her eyes, usually alight with unspoken thoughts, seemed to pierce the very essence of the question.

"I don't want to lose my cultural identity," she confessed, her voice slightly strained with the weight of her admission. "I come from a community where integration into the mainstream has often meant dilution of our unique practices and beliefs. Medical school and subsequent years of training might demand conformity, but the rich heritage of my roots shapes my perspective on life and healing. I must not lose that."

Silence befell us again as I pondered Soraya's apprehension, grasping her struggle on a deep level.

Beatrice was the third to speak, folding her hands neatly in her lap, her voice as calm and measured as a quiet stream.

"I absolutely cannot lose the pure joy of learning. Right now, each day is filled with new knowledge, intriguing mysteries, and the joys of discovery. I worry that—with time—medicine may become just a routine, that the demands and bureaucracy of healthcare will snuff out this spark that drives my curiosity and happiness."

Her words made me think of the mechanization of passions: a common casualty in professional realms. This thought caused a pang of anxiety to ripple through me like a stone disturbing a pond's placid surface.

Finally, it was my turn. I paused, reflecting on the personal sacrifices often associated with a career in medicine: long hours, relentless stress, and emotional tolls. I was nervous about these, too, but something else tugged at my heart more persistently.

"I... I'm afraid of losing empathy," I finally said, my voice barely above a whisper, yet it drew all eyes toward me. "In the grind of medical routines, sickness, and suffering, I cannot stop seeing patients as people, much like what Beatrice said. My empathy is something I never want to lose, no matter the pressures or challenges. I would sooner leave medicine before losing that side of me."

Dr. Altamura smiled softly at us, his gaze thoughtful.

"These fears," he began, his voice enveloping the circle, "are not mere personal anxieties or signs of weakness. Contrary to what many people think, they are powerful reminders of what makes us human and what can make us exceptional as physicians. Family medicine, in its purest essence, isn't just about treating diseases; it's about touching lives profoundly and personally and connecting with our communities. Never lose sight of these fears because they anchor us to the very core of our humanity."

His words resonated with us, a beacon that would guide us through our upcoming years in residency and beyond into our careers. As the discussion wrapped up and we stood to stretch our legs, I felt a renewed sense of purpose. The journey would be long and arduous, but as long as we held onto what we feared to lose, we could all genuinely make a difference. Empathy would be my guiding star—unwavering and luminous—in the pursuit of taking care of people.

"Promise me this," Dr. Altamura said seriously as we assembled in the cabin. "Promise me that you will always look out for one another as brothers and sisters. The bond you will develop with one another in your training will be unrivaled, and you must cherish it."

As the sky darkened, Dr. Altamura suggested we head back to shore. He started the engine again, and we began the journey back. We all seemed more relaxed and at ease, having had the chance to unwind and reflect on our training before starting work in the clinic and hospital soon. As darkness enveloped us, the stars emerged, shimmering above us like distant lanterns. It spoke of the vastness of the universe, reminding us that our worries and struggles were small in comparison. Eventually, we made our way back to Frieden Bay, our hearts full and minds at peace. Our journey on *The Albatross* had brought us closer, not just as friends, but as individuals who understood the challenges and rewards of a life dedicated to serving others.

As we arrived back at the docks, Dr. Altamura thanked us for joining him on the boat ride. He reminded us to take care of ourselves and keep life in perspective, no matter how busy our schedules may be. Before I could disembark, Dr. Altamura called out to me to wait. I waved at my colleagues as they left.

"I wanted to talk to you one-on-one, if you don't mind," he said.

I nodded eagerly, curious to hear what he had to say.

"You know, my grandfather was a former Navy officer," he said, sipping a beer he pulled out of his cooler. "He was a true seafarer and passed down his love for boating to me."

I tilted my head, wanting to hear more about his family history.

"He would take me out on the water every chance he got. I remember feeling like I was on top of the world, sailing together with him," Dr. Altamura continued, his eyes reflecting a mixture of sadness and longing.

Suddenly, he grew quiet, lost in his memories. After a moment, he cleared his throat and continued.

"But one day, a terrible storm hit. My grandfather was out at sea when it happened. The waves were fierce, the winds howling. I never saw him again."

I could see the pain in his eyes as he recounted the events of that tragic day.

"The storm destroyed his boat, tearing it to shreds. It was a cruel twist of fate that took him from me," Dr. Altamura muttered, staring out at the sea from which we just returned.

I stood in stunned silence, imagining the horror of that fateful day. I reached out to comfort him, but he shook his head, signaling he was not finished.

"His death shook me to my core, but it also ignited a fire within me. I dedicated a large part of my life to studying the sea, to understanding its power and beauty," he said, a steely resolve in his gaze. "I guess you could call it my side job when I'm not seeing patients."

As he spoke, I could see the determination and passion that fueled his work. It was clear that his grandfather's untimely death had left a lasting impact on him, shaping the man he had become.

"Thankfully, I have had no accidents yet," he said, knocking heavily on the dock. "You cannot prevent all negative outcomes from occurring; you just do your best to maintain control of what you can control."

With that, Dr. Altamura bid me farewell. I stood in awe and admiration of this remarkable man. His boat may be named after the majestic albatross, but he was the one who possessed the wings to uplift spirits and heal souls, navigating the treacherous waters of medicine with grace and compassion.

I left the dock feeling grateful for the experience and the valuable lessons I had learned from Dr. Altamura. All the same, my steps felt heavy as I crossed the town back to my apartment, like I had lead bricks in my shoes. Even though I did feel more optimistic about starting my clinical work, a nagging feeling of self-doubt persisted. As I ruminated on that self-doubt, it seemed as though my footsteps echoed into the night, closely followed by the sound of identical footsteps just behind me.

CHAPTER SIX

A Frail Man Lying on a Bed

> *Nevertheless, bold fools continue to enter and re-enter the hermetic realm in perpetuum, making the decision each time to do so. It was one of these fools.*

Following the weekend spent with Dr. Altamura and the other residents, I took my first plunge into the deep end of clinical medicine. Monday morning arrived, and with it, I arrived at the Alta Vista Primary Care Center bright and early, eager to begin my shift. Walking through the clinic doors, I was nervous about starting as a rookie doctor. I had spent years studying and preparing for this moment, and now I was finally going to put my skills to the test. The senior residents warmly greeted my co-interns and me and took the four of us under their wings, showing us the ropes and guiding us through seeing patients.

With Isaiah's help, I learned the basics of using the electronic health record, including how to view my day's schedule. My six patients were a diverse group, ranging from a young child with a fever to an elderly man with diabetes and chronic heart failure. As I met with each patient, I listened carefully to their concerns, asked probing questions, and performed a thorough physical examination. Each encounter increased my confidence in my abilities and strengthened my connection with the patients.

One patient in particular stood out to me: a young woman who had been struggling with anxiety and depression for years. As she poured out her heart to me, I could see the pain of defeat and the cautious hope in her eyes. I listened intently, offering words of reassurance and a treatment plan that included psychotherapy and medication. By the end of our appointment, she thanked me for taking the time to listen and understand her struggles. The therapeutic alliance seemed to benefit her more than anything I had ordered for her.

Throughout the day, I was repeatedly amazed by my fellow residents' careful assessments and thoughtful plans. They worked tirelessly to provide the best care possible for each patient, going above and beyond to make sure everyone received the help they needed. I was inspired by their commitment to their patients, even when they were unsure of how to manage specific medical issues. With the wisdom of our senior residents providing invaluable at-the-elbow support, our team was unstoppable.

As I left the clinic that evening, I felt invigorated and motivated by a deeper understanding of the power of medicine. I was ready to continue my journey as a family medicine resident, knowing that, with the support of my colleagues and the guidance of my mentors, I could make a real difference in the future. My first day's work vivified me so much that I woke up early the next morning to pre-chart and put together my care plans before seeing my patients. This experience of having more autonomy in decision-making was much more gratifying than being a student.

Isaiah served as my senior resident for the next two days. His calm and collected demeanor made me feel fortunate to have him guiding me through my initial days in the clinic. We had valuable discussions about clinical pearls and cognitive frameworks he employed to handle complex cases. On my fourth day, I worked directly with the attending physician preceptor without the assistance of a senior resident. Incredibly, I had the privilege of working with Dr. Calisto, a seasoned physician with a wealth of knowledge and experience. From our interactions, I knew I was in capable hands.

The theme of the day was follow-up visits with adults needing chronic disease management. Dr. Calisto guided me through the best practices for common chronic diseases, such as chronic hypertension, diabetes mellitus, and hypothyroidism. He emphasized the importance of thorough history-taking, physical examination, and the appropriate use of diagnostic tests and treatment options. We discussed a beneficial clinical guidelines article summarizing evidence-based strategies for managing chronic kidney disease in the context of diabetes over lunchtime. I absorbed everything he taught me like a sponge, ready to learn as much as possible from him.

Toward the end of the afternoon, I saw an otherwise healthy man in his sixties named Bernard James who had a strange complaint: sudden and episodic shortness of breath. His medical history was unremarkable, and he had no known major risk factors for heart disease or chronic lung conditions.

"When did this start?" I inquired after introducing myself and sitting on a stool near my computer in the exam room.

"It's been happening off and on for probably three or four months," Mr. James replied, scratching his head as he tried remembering the day he first noticed the odd symptom. "It doesn't seem to matter what I'm doing, either. I jog regularly, and occasionally, I'll get a sharp twinge in the middle of my chest."

"Any pain in your legs with exercise?" I asked, mentally ticking things off of my differential diagnosis. "Have you ever had pain anywhere else since the shortness of breath started?"

"I don't get any pain in my legs, but sometimes, there's a sharp pain that always goes away fast in my mid-back," he thoughtfully answered, pointing to his thoracic spine. "It's so weird when it happens."

"Does your shortness of breath worsen when you get that pain?" I leaned in closer, becoming increasingly curious.

"Hmmm... You know, I think it does. I never thought about it that way, but I have to slow down when that happens."

After collecting more information from Mr. James, I performed a targeted physical examination, which included listening to his heart and lungs, checking for costovertebral angle and paraspinal muscle tenderness, and thoroughly examining his abdomen. Despite my evaluation, I could not identify any apparent source of his symptoms. Before returning to our workroom to present the case to Dr. Calisto, I jotted down a few notes to organize my thoughts.

"No new medications," I reported, staring down at my list. "No modifying factors."

"What about the physical exam findings?" Dr. Calisto asked, puzzled by the history. "Vital signs?"

"Heart and lungs normal. Abdomen's soft and non-tender with normal bowel sounds. No CVA or paraspinal tenderness to palpation or percussion," I related, now looking up at the ceiling as I tried to solve the mystery in my head. "Normal vitals, normal respiratory rate, heart rate 93, O2 sats 91%."

Dr. Calisto leaned far back in his chair, rubbing his forehead hard as the gears in his brain turned feverishly.

"I know that his O2 sats and heart rate are technically 'normal,' but they seem a little off for someone at sea level who's at rest," he observed, pursing his lips. "Humor me with a quick workup, given that we can do some things here in the clinic."

Per Dr. Calisto's recommendations, I ordered a chest X-ray with anterior-posterior and lateral views and an electrocardiogram to rule out immediate concerns. While our medical assistants and technicians performed the studies, I saw my last patient: a young woman needing a refill on her birth control pills. After I sent her to the front to check out, I returned to the workroom to find his EKG in front of my computer and Dr. Calisto looking over the X-ray images, his nose almost touching his monitor.

"Come over here and read this X-ray with me," he beckoned me over, patting a chair right next to him.

I did what he had asked, parking myself in the chair to his right. He moved back from the screen to allow me to click through the two images we had. I ran through the mnemonic I had for reviewing plain radiographs of the chest, starting with the airway and then working my way to the lung fields, heart, diaphragm, and finally, the bones.

"I don't see anything abnormal here," I concluded, quickly scanning through the images again to make sure I did not miss anything obvious. "No pleural effusions. No large pneumothorax. The right hemidiaphragm is riding a little high, but that's about it."

"I agree with you," Dr. Calisto remarked, unable to conceal his pride. "Now, let's check out the EKG."

I reached across from where we were sitting to bring the red and white paper to where we could look at it together.

"Hmmm..." I vocalized, going through the rate, rhythm, axis, and wave progression on the EKG. "Everything is basically normal. I do see slight sinus arrhythmia in some of the leads, but nothing that looks grossly abnormal."

"Are you sure about that?" Dr. Calisto asked, pulling out a pen to point to the right side of the paper. "That looks funky in the precordial leads. It actually looks like some depressions in the ST segments with a possible T-wave inversion in V2."

"Right heart strain," I whispered as a cardiology lecture from medical school played back in my head.

"Exactly! I have a bad feeling about this," he disclosed. "Let's grab the ultrasound machine. We need to check on something to figure out the final plan for today."

It was 5:30 pm, and most of the clinic staff had gone home for the day. Dr. Calisto and I hastily marched to the procedure room, where we kept the ultrasound machine. Wheeling it over, we headed into Mr. James' room, introducing Dr. Calisto as we entered.

"Hello, sir," Dr. Calisto animatedly said, reaching out to shake Mr. James' hand. "It's nice to meet you. Your doctor and I discussed what brought you in today and reviewed your chest X-ray and EKG findings. While the chest X-ray was completely normal, I have concerns about your EKG. It showed some strain along the right side of your heart, which most often happens when there is an increase in pressure in the blood vessels in your lungs."

"H-how does that happen?" Mr. James stammered, demanding to know more.

"I'm worried you could have a clot in your lungs," he answered, keeping an even tone. "What we can do for you this afternoon is check your legs for clots using this machine over here."

"Okay, let's do that," Mr. James stated, exhaling heavily under the weight of a new anxiety. "What do I need to do?"

We informed Mr. James that he would need to remove his jeans and cover his legs with a drape. After giving him time to undress, we returned to the room and had him lie flat on the exam bed. Positioning his left leg like a frog's leg, we started the point-of-care exam with the ultrasound, using a linear probe to track his veins from the popliteal vein behind his knee up to the common femoral vein around his groin. Dr. Calisto provided pointers to me about how to appropriately test for deep vein thrombosis by compressing the veins at regular intervals. As we got to his groin, we found no obvious clots in the veins of his left leg.

"Now, I want you to repeat the same exam on the other side," Dr. Calisto instructed, handing me the ultrasound probe.

After wiping the transmission gel off his left leg and repositioning him on the right side, I started searching for a clot in the deeper veins of his right leg. After fumbling with the probe for thirty seconds, I finally got the right popliteal vein in view. I closely studied the grayscale image on the screen attached to the machine. Applying pressure to the vein revealed a positive finding.

"He's non-compressible at the right pop," I quietly reported to Dr. Calisto to avoid alarming the patient until I was done with my examination. "I'm going to start tracking superiorly."

I applied external pressure with the probe every one or two centimeters, finding that all the veins would not collapse.

"I think we've seen enough," Dr. Calisto said, nodding at me as he grabbed some paper towels to wipe the gel off Mr. James' right leg. "Mr. James, we've found evidence of what we call a DVT, or deep vein thrombosis, in your right leg. I strongly suspect that this clot has traveled to your lungs and is causing a pulmonary embolism, which would explain your shortness of breath and intermittent back pain."

"Wow," Mr. James uttered, scrambling to sit up on the exam bed. "What do we need to do now?"

I explained to Mr. James that we would need to get him over to the emergency department at our hospital across the street for further evaluation, including a special CT scan of his lungs that would show the blood vessels. Dr. Calisto called over to the charge nurse in the emergency department to give notice of his impending arrival and arrange for transportation to the unit. Once the patient was handed off to the emergency medical technicians, Dr. Calisto and I collected our bags and headed to the hospital. Over cups of coffee we picked up from the physician's lounge, we discussed the incidence of these issues in the local population and what resources were available in Frieden Bay to get patients timely treatment.

"When I was in residency," Dr. Calisto remarked, blowing on his piping hot coffee, "I had a mentor who was like a walking encyclopedia—the smartest guy I had ever met. He always recited an adage when we worked in the clinic: 'Enigmatic cases are more likely due to atypical presentations of common diseases than typical presentations of rare diseases.' If Mr. James does have a clot in one or both of his lungs, it proves my mentor right."

That's helpful, I thought. *That's like how medical students are warned about not chasing zebras when they hear hoofbeats.*

Once the patient was transported and placed in a room in the emergency department, Dr. Calisto and I went by to check on him before ordering some tests: blood work to check on parameters like his blood counts, coagulation factors, signs of heart damage and failure, and kidney function; a full venous ultrasound scan to ascertain the extent of the DVT; and a CT angiogram to check for a pulmonary embolism. With everything in process, Dr. Calisto and I took a moment to take a breather.

"Excellent work today," he complimented me, facing me from his swivel chair. "I appreciate you going above and beyond for your patient today."

"I should say the same to you," I grinned widely before yawning. "I learned so much about managing outpatient issues that require escalating care on the spot. Plus, Mr. James got the best care possible from both of us."

"It's getting pretty late," he said, glancing down at his watch. "I know you're scheduled to work with Dr. Coffman on the inpatient teaching service tomorrow. Since you have to wake up early, why don't you head home and get some sleep? I'll stay back and do the admission to follow up on the test results. I will message you all with the important updates."

Knowing it was not a good idea to protest such generosity, I simply nodded at Dr. Calisto before collecting my leather laptop bag, throwing away the paper cup my coffee was in, and then leaving the hospital. On the way home, I reflected on how much I learned about patient care today and how much I would learn tomorrow when I followed up with Mr. James on the wards, fully realizing the continuum of care on which our specialty was built.

HALF-CONSCIOUS IN BED, THE JARRING NOTES OF MY alarm jerked me fully awake, serving as a cruel reminder that I had only slept for five hours. Despite how exhausted I felt, I was chomping at the bit to get over to the hospital to check on

Mr. James and work with our inpatient team. I shook off the sluggishness of sleep deprivation and made my way to my bathroom to shower before donning my blue scrubs embroidered with the Alta Vista logo. With my bag in hand, I started off on my early morning drive to the hospital.

In addition to meeting up with our Associate Program Director in the hospitalist workroom, I also joined Brett Erickson and Gabrielle Carmichael, a second and third-year resident in our program, respectively. They welcomed me to the inpatient teaching service and handed me a list of the patients we had on service for the day. After receiving my assignment for the day, I scanned the list and found Mr. James' name toward the bottom. Clicking through his chart in the electronic health record to understand what had transpired since I last saw him, I discovered that his blood work results were unremarkable; his ultrasound showed a massive clot traveling all along the venous system of the right leg; and that his CT angiogram showed extensive pulmonary emboli in the left lung.

"Did you see the incidental finding on the radiologist's report?" Dr. Coffman inquired, noticing that I was reviewing the results from overnight. "Check this out."

We opened the report and read through what Dr. Coffman had mentioned. There was a note about a two-centimeter irregular lesion on the inferior left side of the diaphragm that was enhanced with the iodinated contrast used for the chest angiography.

"I'm not sure what that is," Dr. Coffman admitted. "But, we need to investigate it with additional imaging. Dr. Calisto also put in his history and physical note that this patient had no history of recent travel, no family history of clotting disorders, and no new medications or illnesses. We have not identified a clear provocation for this DVT yet, but based on the huge size of it, I suspect something is going on."

Right out of the gate, I followed up with Mr. James, who was on the second floor in our progressive care unit. Recognizing someone he had already met, his face brightened as I entered his room, which had a beautiful view of the mountains to the west of town.

"Mr. James, how are you feeling, sir?" I initiated the conversation, casting a cursory glance at his pulse oximetry readings.

"I've been better, but God was watching over me when he guided me to see you and Dr. Calisto yesterday," he told me, an iota of shame visible on his brow. "If I hadn't, I could've died at home."

"I'm glad you came in to see us in the clinic, too," I responded reassuringly. "You are now on the right medications to manage this issue over the long haul, particularly that blood thinner called apixaban we started last night."

He smiled, laughing nervously with gratitude for the immediate care.

"Well, what's the plan for today?"

"I'm glad you asked," I said, preparing myself to discuss the CT findings. "You probably heard about the little clots we found in your left lung. We found something else on the left underside of your diaphragm—the dome-shaped muscle that helps you breathe."

He stared at me with a curious expression.

"What is it?"

"We aren't sure yet. Apart from continuing your blood thinner, the main plan for today is to get a CT scan of your abdomen to figure out what that spot on the diaphragm is and whether there are other spots like it around your other internal organs."

His discontent with the news was apparent as I made steady eye contact with him.

"Okay, let's do it. Let's get that scan going."

Immediately after checking on him, I ordered the CT scan with Brett's assistance. He informed me that these imaging studies were typically done quickly at this hospital and that I should follow up on the results after we finished rounds. After reviewing and discussing all sixteen patients during table rounds, I sat down in the workroom to finish my progress notes and discharge summaries and to check for any updates on patients. A little red icon drew my attention to an abnormal result, and when I clicked on it, I was pleased to see that Brett was correct about the CT scan. I had to stop after only a few words because the radiologic interpretation was very lengthy.

I have never seen anything like this from a CT, I thought, steeling my nerves to push forward.

"Is that for Mr. James?" Gabrielle checked in with the air of a seasoned senior resident.

"Yeah, I'm a little overwhelmed by everything the radiologist wrote," I confessed self-consciously.

Gabrielle and I read the report together, and our jaws dropped by the end.

"Oh my God!" Gabrielle exclaimed, taken aback by the findings. "He's riddled with mets. This is peritoneal carcinomatosis. We need to get oncology and palliative care on board right away."

I got on the phone to consult with the two teams while Gabrielle brought Dr. Coffman up to speed on the foreboding discovery. After I finished consulting with the oncologist, he requested that we order specialized blood work to test for several different tumor markers to narrow down the list of possible primary tumors. Though it pained me, I immediately went to Mr. James' room and updated him.

"T-tumors in my abdomen?" he stammered as bemusement deepened the furrows along his forehead. "How could this happen?"

With difficulty, I swallowed the thick saliva in my mouth.

"We don't know why this happened," I disclosed, nearly mumbling.

I did not have a definite answer for him. Never before had I seen a human look so defeated and anguished. The skin of his wrinkled brow stretched in vexation, making him look haggard.

"Did I do this to myself?" Mr. James asked, desperately searching my eyes for any semblance of an answer. "Was this the result of my past mistakes in life?"

The sinking sensation I felt deep in my chest kept me from uttering a single word for several seconds.

"It's unlikely we will ever know for sure why this happened," I confessed, meeting his gaze. "Just know that you were not solely responsible for this."

I became acutely aware of the dryness of my mouth and tingling in my fingers as I bowed my head, sharing a contemplative silence with this gentleman. We exchanged unfeigned looks of pain before I clasped his hand and left the room.

The next morning, the oncologist stopped by the workroom to discuss the lab results and his management recommendations.

"Most of the tumor markers were negative," Dr. Fareed Mohammed stated. "However, one came back markedly elevated: CA 19-9. Based on the size and extent of the tumor on the pancreas, I suspect that this started as a silent pancreatic head adenocarcinoma."

"Damn," I uttered as I took a seat, resting my head on my hand. "This isn't curable, then."

"His prognosis is extremely poor," he frowned, confirming my suspicion. "Palliative chemo may be an option if he develops intractable pain, but I would not put him through surgical debulking or curative chemotherapy. Based on what I have seen—and we don't even have the PET scan yet—I would estimate he may only have one or two months left at best."

With this bleak news directly from the expert, I had no choice but to talk to Mr. James.

"Pancreatic cancer..." he whispered, too dumbfounded to communicate at an average volume. "That's what Alex Trebek died from, huh? I guess that means I'm a goner."

I had pulled a chair up to his bedside before breaking the terrible news. I needed him to know that we were there for him, to support him with every decision he would need to make.

"The oncologist doesn't think there is any reasonable possibility of curing this," I reported, maintaining a comforting tone. "But, we can make this easier for you. A doctor with the palliative care team should be by later today to discuss supportive care options with you."

"How long do I have?" he asked with a profound seriousness. "What do I tell my children?"

"One to two months," I said, tentative in my response.

That night, I slept horribly, tossing and turning constantly as the conversation with Mr. James replayed repeatedly in my head. Even still, I was not about to throw in the towel on him; there was still work to be done. When I arrived the next morning, Gabrielle turned to me from her computer screen with a doleful expression.

"He popped a fever last night," Gabrielle updated me as I sat at my computer. "The night team ordered a chest X-ray, and it shows that he developed hospital-acquired pneumonia. Given that he met sepsis criteria, he's currently on piperacillin-tazobactam and vancomycin. We still do not have a clear pathogen; the respiratory culture is pending. His troponin level bumped a little, which is probably demand-mediated myocardial ischemia."

This is not good, I thought as I rubbed my head. *The infection is placing stress on his heart. We have to get this under control soon before things get worse. This could easily kill him.*

Just as she finished her update, Dr. Coffman entered the room with a grave expression.

"I just got a call from Mr. James' nurse," he said flatly. "He's delirious now. I don't think he has much longer."

Later that morning, the social worker on our team came by to let us know that Mr. James' son and daughter wanted to have a family meeting to discuss the next steps in their father's care. I knew this was a crucial moment for the family because they would have to make some difficult decisions about their father's future.

I sat down with Mr. James' children, Tom and Rebecca, in a small conference room on the second floor of the hospital. They were both clearly distressed, their faces filled with worry and sadness. I tried to reassure them as I explained the options available for their father.

"Given your father's deteriorating condition, we have a few choices to consider," I began. "We can continue with aggressive treatment with antibiotics and medications to raise his blood pressure, which may prolong his life but may also put him through more pain and suffering. Or we can focus on palliative care, ensuring that he is as comfortable and pain-free as possible in his final days."

Tom looked at me with a troubled expression.

"But we don't want to give up on our dad. We want to do everything we can to help him get through this."

Rebecca nodded in agreement, tears welling up in her eyes.

"We can't just give up on him."

I could see the love and desperation in their eyes, and my heart ached for them. It was never easy to make decisions like these, especially when it involved a loved one's life. Nevertheless, I knew my duty was to guide them through this difficult process.

"I understand your feelings completely, but we must also consider what your father would want," I said gently. "At this point, he can no longer make decisions for himself. It's important to consider what he would want in this situation."

Tom sighed, running a hand through his hair in frustration.

"I don't know what he would want. We never talked about this kind of stuff."

Rebecca wiped away her tears and spoke up.

"But we can't just let him suffer. We have to do what's best for him, even if it's hard for us to accept."

I could see the resolve in her eyes, and I knew she was trying to be strong for her father's sake. I admired her courage and knew that whatever decision they made would be in their father's best interest.

After a long discussion, Tom and Rebecca finally reached a decision. They chose to focus on supportive care for their father, ensuring that he was kept comfortable in his final days. It was a difficult choice, but they knew it was right for him.

I held their hands and offered them my support.

"You're making a brave and selfless decision for your father. He will be proud of you for choosing to ease his suffering."

As we left the conference room and returned to Mr. James' room, I saw acceptance settle over Tom and Rebecca. They had made a difficult choice, one that would protect their father's comfort and dignity in his final moments. As I finished rounding on my last patient for the day, I felt the exhaustion clinging to my limbs. It had been a long and tiring day, filled with a rollercoaster of highs and lows. Just as I was about to head home, Mr. James' nurse approached me somberly.

"I don't think Mr. James will make it until the morning," Angelique said solemnly. "Before you go home, will you sit with him as he passes? It would mean the world to him. I can join you."

For a moment, I despised myself because my mind was consumed by how much I wanted instead to sprawl out on the couch and binge-watch another stand-up comedy special. However, I knew it was the fatigue talking. I re-centered, took a deep breath, remembered how important this choice was for Mr. James, and slowly nodded.

The air inside the room felt dense, filled with the faint scent of antiseptic and the aura of impending loss. As I pushed open the door, I was met with the sight of a frail man lying on a bed, hooked up to numerous whirring machines that breathed life into his weakened body. Plastic tubes snaked across the room, monitoring his vital signs and minimizing discomfort in his final moments.

Approaching his bedside, I reintroduced myself softly, knowing he lacked the strength to respond. Settling into chairs beside him, Angelique and I began to speak, our voices gentle and soothing. It felt as though time stood still, an interlude where only whispers of relief filled the space. As the minutes turned into hours, I noticed the changing rhythm of Mr. James' breathing. It grew shallower, with longer pauses between each breath, until finally, it ceased altogether. Once marked by worry, his face now bore the serenity that comes only with release. It was over.

Mr. James had taken his final breath and slipped away from this world. A profound silence settled over the room, the reality of his departure sinking in as we sat there. Slowly, the nurse and I unhurriedly rose to our feet. My mind wandered as I thought about Mr. James' life and his legacy. The weight of his absence hung around me, a reminder of the fragility of existence and the importance of human connection.

As I said goodbye to Mr. James, I vowed to honor his memory and the lessons he taught me. I would continue to care for those in need and always remember the impact a kind word or gesture can have on someone suffering. As Angelique and I made our way out of the room, I reflected on the significance of that time spent by Mr. James' side. In those moments, I had been a physician and a companion. I witnessed the final chapter of a man's life, making sure he was not alone during this sacred passage as his book snapped shut.

CHAPTER SEVEN

Away from the Shore

> *The unfortunate reality is that a rational mind does not readily make the decision; it is made by those who have drunk too deeply the waters of an oneiric fantasy.*

About three months had passed since my first inpatient rotation, and I could sense my clinical skills were getting sharper by the minute. Vincent and I joked with each other that we already looked wiser in our short time as residents. Between my shifts in the hospital and clinic, I worked on the apartment, making it a more desirable place to live. I started to notice how difficult it was to get in touch with Mr. Haron when something came up; it always seemed like he was traveling for business when I needed to reach him.

After long days at work, I habitually stopped by The Beacon for a drink, indulging in local ales and other alcoholic beverages. Dr. Altamura would often be at the bar, sitting in the same place he was when I first met him. He and I would talk for hours about many different topics, ranging from politics to art. Every time we chatted, we had a great time and learned more about each other, and he gave me some of the most valuable life advice I had ever received. Dr. Altamura was an inspiration to me, and I looked to him more and more frequently for his sagacious guidance.

In my continuity clinic, I now had three pregnant patients on my panel. One of them was Claire Galbraith, a twenty-one-year-old first-time mother with a history of opioid use disorder. I was seeing her for her prenatal visits. Claire was a sweet and diffident young woman with a troubled past. She had been in and out of rehab for her opioid use and was focused on turning her life around for the sake of her unborn child.

When she first came into the office, she was hesitant to talk about her past, but as time went on, she began to open up to me and talk about her struggles. During our visits, I could see the fear and uncertainty in Claire's eyes as we discussed her pregnancy and the risks associated with opioid use while pregnant. I reassured her that we would do everything we could to ensure a healthy pregnancy and delivery for both her and her baby.

As the weeks went by, Claire became gradually more anxious about the upcoming birth of her child. She confided in me about her fears of relapsing and not being able to care for her baby properly. I listened to her concerns and offered her my support and guidance. During one of her prenatal visits, Claire broke down in tears and admitted that she was still having cravings for fentanyl. She was ashamed and embarrassed, but I assured her that she was not alone and that we would work together to get her the help she needed.

I referred Claire to a support group for women struggling with addiction and urged her to attend regular counseling sessions to help manage her cravings. During our appointments, I suggested a medication to help her manage her addiction, but she said she was not ready to do that yet. Despite her fears and obstacles, Claire was determined not to use fentanyl for the sake of her baby. She attended all her appointments and followed her treatment plan diligently. I could see the willpower in her eyes as she prepared for the birth of her child.

Claire had been on a rollercoaster of emotions since she found out she was pregnant. She had dealt with addiction in the past, but she had been sober for over a year before she found out she was expecting. The news had brought her so much joy and hope for the future, but it had also brought back memories of her past difficulties with substance use.

I noticed a strange, new scar on her lip during her next prenatal visit.

"How did you get that?" I asked non-confrontationally, gesturing to her lower lip where her lipstick failed to conceal the defect fully.

"I don't know," she said, looking toward the wall. "I must have fallen or something a while back. I sometimes bite my lips."

My intuition told me she was being deceptive, but I needed to maintain rapport with her to give her the best care possible. When Claire finally talked to me about her relapse about four weeks later, my heart ached for her. I had seen firsthand the devastating effects addiction could have on a person's life, and I was determined to help her through this difficult time. We sat down in the clinic, and I listened as she poured her heart out to me, tears streaming down her face.

"I just couldn't resist," she admitted, her voice barely above a whisper. "The cravings were so strong, and I felt like I had no control over them. So, I ended up smoking blues. That's how I got this scar on my lip; I burnt myself on a pipe."

"Claire," I said to her without judgment in my communication. "We're going to keep you and your baby safe. You showed me courage today by telling me about what happened. That honesty is going to allow me to help you more directly."

I knew all too well the power addiction could have over a person. I explained to her the options we had for managing her substance use disorder during her pregnancy, including the use of buprenorphine to help curb her cravings. I could see the fear and shame in her eyes, but I reassured her that we would get through this together.

Over the next few weeks, we worked closely together to develop a plan for Claire's recovery. She started taking the buprenorphine under close supervision and continued with the support group and counseling program. It was a long and difficult road, but Claire was committed to doing whatever it took to give her baby the best possible start in life. As her pregnancy progressed, I saw a gradual transformation in Claire: she seemed more confident and hopeful, and her eyes sparkled with a newfound sense of purpose.

Apart from her substance use concerns, Claire also worried about developing pre-eclampsia—a potentially fatal pregnancy complication characterized by high blood pressure—because her mother and grandmother both developed this when they were pregnant. Shortly after I met her, we discussed a plan for her to check her blood pressure at home if she had a headache, pain in the right upper part of her abdomen, vision changes, or other concerning symptoms. As a precaution, I also started her on low-dose aspirin per official guidelines, which was shown to prevent pre-eclampsia.

When she was about thirty-eight weeks pregnant, I received an urgent message alert in the electronic health record while completing one of my office visit notes: "Doctor—this is Claire. I need you to call me ASAP. My blood pressure is very high, and my vision is blurry."

Oh no, I thought, my chest tightening. *This sounds like pre-eclampsia. I need to call her right now.*

After getting Claire on the phone, she frantically reported that her home blood pressure readings had been in the 160s/110s multiple times. I advised her that we could handle this in the hospital and instructed her partner to drive her to the obstetrical triage for evaluation. After hanging up, I immediately called Dr. Mose, who frequently worked in the Labor and Delivery unit at Alta Vista and was scheduled to be the on-call family physician for the service that day. I discussed the case with her, and she agreed that Claire's symptoms were concerning for pre-eclampsia with severe features and that induction of labor would likely be necessary.

The urgency and seriousness of the situation weighed heavily on my mind as I drove over to the obstetrical triage to meet Claire. When I arrived at the hospital and got to the unit on the third floor, I found Claire in Triage Room #3, where she sat bawling out of fear for her baby. I could see the trepidation in her eyes as she explained how her blood pressure readings had steadily risen over the past few days and how the blurry vision started about an hour before she sent me the patient portal message.

Dr. Mose and I performed a targeted physical examination, reviewed the tracing from the cardiotocography, used our bedside ultrasound machine to ascertain the baby's position in the uterus, started intravenous magnesium sulfate and labetalol after confirming her elevated blood pressure reading ten minutes after the first, and then ordered urine and blood tests to check for evidence of pre-eclampsia. After conferring, we decided the best course of action was to admit her immediately for further evaluation and management. Pre-eclampsia was a potentially life-threatening condition for both Claire and her baby, and we needed to act fast to prevent complications.

Once the nurses moved Claire into her new room in the Labor and Delivery unit, I checked on her once more and told her I would be there to monitor her progress overnight. Afterward, I relocated to the call room on the other side of the unit. I accessed Claire's chart in the electronic health record to review her lab test results. The findings were striking: she had massive amounts of protein in her urine and an elevated creatinine level. These results signaled kidney dysfunction, and taking these findings together with her blurry vision and markedly elevated blood pressure readings, it was clear that she did have pre-eclampsia with severe features.

Even though I would have to cancel my clinic sessions tomorrow to be present for her delivery, I felt responsible for Claire's care. I was committed to doing everything in my power to help her through this difficult time and see her newborn. After closing the chart, I returned to her room to explain the risks and potential complications of pre-eclampsia and to reassure her that we were going to do everything we could to keep her and her baby safe. Over the next few hours, we closely monitored Claire's condition. She was started on antihypertensive medication with good effect, and her blood pressure readings stayed more consistently below 140/90. I checked in on her regularly, answering her questions and providing her with the support and reassurance she needed during this stressful time.

Around the same time, Dr. Mose and I chatted about our plan to induce her labor since the only permanent solution to the pre-eclampsia was the delivery of the baby. Her first cervical exam when she got to the hospital showed that her cervix was not favorable for delivery just yet. Given that information and what we knew about her contraction pattern, we opted for intravaginal misoprostol, which would help to soften her cervix and prepare her for a vaginal delivery. After her nurse placed the medication for us, we knew we were on the right track to having a successful and hopefully uneventful birth.

As I was finishing up with a labor progress note, I saw Beatrice walking down the hall with Dr. Santiago Lucero, the on-call obstetrician-gynecologist for the evening.

"Hey there, Bea," I waved to her from the central workstation. "How's your shift with Dr. Lucero going?"

"It's going great!" she responded, sitting beside me. "Dr. Lucero is a fantastic teacher. We had three deliveries earlier today, including one C-section. He gauged where I was skill-wise the whole time. But…"

Beatrice stopped mid-sentence, clearly conflicted about what she would say next.

"But, what?" I prompted.

"But I just feel like I should know more than I do by this point in our training."

"Bea, come on," I tittered, nudging her to get her to loosen up. "It's October of intern year, for crying out loud. I've seen you in action: you're doing wonderfully. I'm not kidding when I say that you outshine a lot of the seniors. You are exceptional, and I know the faculty see it, too. Dr. Calisto even said as much in passing last week."

"He did?" she turned toward me with more energy in her voice. "That's very flattering. It is good to know he thinks highly of me."

"We just have to trust in the process. That's what they told us when we started in July."

Beatrice's shoulders fully relaxed, and with contentment now visible in her mannerisms, she leaned back in her chair and pulled up the electronic health record.

"I forgot to ask earlier, but why are you over here?" she probed, accessing the list of patients on the unit. "Is it for this patient?"

"Yes," I confirmed, glancing over her shoulder. "She's one of my clinic patients. Claire is a twenty-one-year-old primip we admitted for pre-eclampsia with severe features. Severe-range pressures at home with blurry vision. Tons of protein in her urine. She bumped her creatinine to a whopping 2.8 here, probably the highest I've seen so far."

"That sounds scary," Beatrice commented, noticing her urine protein and serum creatinine levels. "Any other problems during this pregnancy?"

"Just fentanyl use. I've had her on buprenorphine for a while now, and she's been sta–."

Before I could finish my sentence, Claire's nurse rushed over to us with a wide-eyed expression.

"Doctors, I need your help now! Ms. Galbraith just started seizing after her blood pressure spiked to 200/130 just before she was due for her next dose of labetalol."

"Is the mag still running?" I asked the nurse before jumping from my chair and running to the room.

"I'll join you," Beatrice called out, trailing just a few feet behind me.

I dashed into Claire's room and witnessed what the nurse was describing: a tonic-clonic seizure. Two other nurses had made their way over already and were helping to prevent injury from the patient's flailing limbs. Without hesitation, I confirmed her magnesium orders and added as-needed lorazepam for refractory seizures. Beatrice and I worked quickly and efficiently to stabilize her, all the while trying to keep calm in the face of a life-threatening situation.

"I need you to call Dr. Mose and tell her to come over immediately," I told one of the nurses.

As we continued to work, Dr. Mose ran into the room, nervous lines across her forehead.

"What's the situation here?" she asked me, scanning the room for context clues.

"Tonic-clonic seizure after her blood pressure bounced up to 200/130," I reported. "She's eclamptic now. She seems to be responding well to the magnesium, but we also have some IV lorazepam ready to go if she needs it."

"Once she's stabilized, we have to get her back for a C-section," Dr. Mose said, shaking her head. "Dr. Portinari, could you get in touch with Dr. Lucero and bring him over here right away?"

"Absolutely," Beatrice complied, ripping her nitrile gloves off and throwing them away on her way out the door.

Dr. Mose and I continued to manage Claire while we waited for Dr. Lucero and his expertise. Due to some residual convulsive movements in her extremities, we decided to administer a dose of lorazepam, which resolved the remaining seizure activity. Her vital signs stabilized with additional doses of labetalol and one dose of hydralazine, which lowered her blood pressure to a safe range. Once we had started her on a continuous infusion of magnesium sulfate, Dr. Lucero strode quickly into the room with Beatrice in tow.

"Got it under control now?" he inquired, surveying the monitors and Claire's appearance.

"Seizure's aborted," Dr. Mose reported, helping me adjust Claire's sheets. "Blood pressure's under better control, but this is a tenuous situation."

"We should get her back for a C-section as soon as possible. I have the OR staff preparing Room #5 for us, and the anesthesiologist is on the way there now. Get ready to roll soon."

After we got the clearance to transport, Dr. Mose, Beatrice, her nurse, and I all moved Claire over to the operating room for an emergency cesarean section. Dr. Lucero was already there, giving an update to the anesthesiologist who had just arrived a minute before. The tension in the room was palpable as the team rushed Claire in. Dr. Mose, Beatrice, and I all hurriedly headed for nearby sinks to scrub in for the impending surgery. After grabbing sterile gowns and gloves, we moved inside the operating room, where Dr. Glen Holland, one of the pediatricians, now also stood, ready at the warmer to perform resuscitative interventions on the newborn.

As we filed in, Dr. Lucero shot his eyes over to our group and then pointed at me.

"Instead of having you assist with the C-section, I'll have you join Dr. Holland to help with neonatal resuscitation," he directed calmly. "You know how floppy babies can be after mom gets mag. Another set of hands over there would be helpful if this one needs more support."

I nodded, grabbing some non-sterile nitrile gloves as I stepped over to the warmer. I introduced myself briefly to Dr. Holland before we came up with our strategy to help the baby in case there was no breathing or bradycardia. Dr. Holland kindly ran through all of the equipment available to us in our tiny section of the operating room. After completing the review, I felt more confident about approaching any major issues that might arise after the baby was delivered.

As the surgeon and his assistants worked to deliver the baby, Dr. Holland and I stood by, anxiously awaiting the moment when we would meet Claire's newborn. During the surgery, there were difficulties with the dissection down to the uterus, and Dr. Lucero had to provide several loud but clear instructions to Beatrice to get an optimal window for the delivery.

When the baby was finally born, there was a collective sigh of relief in the room. The infant—a small but overall healthy-appearing baby girl—let out a weak cry as she took her first breaths of air. As the nurses whisked her away to the warmer for further evaluation, Beatrice and I exchanged a look of unspoken relief and gratitude from across the room. Despite the situation's intensity, we worked as a team to save Claire and her baby. It was a testament to the power of collaboration and camaraderie in the fast-paced world of Labor and Delivery.

As expected, the newborn girl's muscle tone was low, but she was moving air well. Dr. Holland and I dried her off, suctioned her mouth and then nose, and administered some blow-by supplemental oxygen to correct a mildly low oxygen saturation level and heart rate. With the baby girl swaddled, I held her in my arms and looked on as she yawned and fidgeted underneath the warm blanket. I felt on top of the world as I gazed upon this new life in front of me. Once Claire came around from the general anesthesia, I introduced her to her newborn daughter.

"Oh my God," Claire cried out hoarsely. "She's beautiful."

As I watched Claire cradle her newborn baby, pride and accomplishment caressed my soul. I had helped her through one of the most difficult times in her life, and together, we had overcome the challenges that stood in her way.

"I did it," she whispered, holding her baby tightly against her chest. "I did it for her."

Reflecting on my time taking care of Claire, I realized that being a physician was more than just diagnosing and treating illnesses. It was about building relationships, offering support, and helping patients like Claire overcome their hurdles. At that moment, I knew that Claire had conquered her demons and emerged victorious. She had vanquished her darkest fears, emerging stronger and more motivated than ever. Looking at the mother and daughter before me, I knew their bond was unbreakable, forged in the fires of adversity and love. Shortly after, Claire's partner came to her side to celebrate the birth of little Anastasia.

As we left the operating room, Beatrice and I shared a moment of mute reflection on the events that had just transpired. We knew we had played a crucial role in helping bring new life into the world, a feeling that would stay with us for a long time. With both of us now drained from the adrenaline rush of that delivery, we veered down a corridor to go to the cafeteria. She seemed visibly shaken about the cesarean section. As we sat at a table, she kept fidgeting with her soda cup, her eyes distant and troubled.

I reached out and placed my hand over hers, wanting to assuage her anxiety.

"Are you okay, Bea?" I asked softly.

She took a deep breath before answering, her voice shaky.

"I just can't stop thinking about the labor management and C-section. What if I had missed something? What if I had made a mistake? I probably would have messed up had I been alone. Having you, Dr. Mose, and Dr. Lucero there to spoon-feed me everything was the only thing keeping me in check."

Her eyes filled with tears as she spoke.

I related to that feeling on some levels. The pressure of being a physician, especially in a high-stress situation, is often horribly overwhelming. I also had my doubts and fears. Seeing Beatrice like this—questioning her abilities after all the hard work she had put into her training so far—broke my heart.

"Bea, you were amazing in there," I stated firmly, trying to convince her of her worth. "Your quick thinking and savvy saved Claire's life. You should be proud of yourself. Plus, we're interns who are still learning. You are not supposed to be a lone wolf on the job, anyway."

She sniffled, wiping away a stray tear.

"I just feel like I'm not cut out for this work, you know? Maybe I'm not as good as I thought I was. Maybe not even as good as others think I am."

I shook my head, strongly disagreeing with her self-doubt.

"No, Bea. You're an incredible physician. Your skills make you stand out. You definitely have what it takes to excel in family medicine."

She looked at me with watery eyes, gratitude and relief evident in her expression.

"Thank you. That means a lot coming from you. You inspire me to be a better physician."

I smiled, touched by her words.

"We make a great team, and being your friend and colleague means everything to me. We're in this together; we'll have each other's backs through the tough times. It's just like Dr. Altamura told us months ago."

Beatrice squeezed my hand, a small smile playing on her lips. "Thank you for always being there for me, for believing in me. I don't know what I would do without you."

I squeezed her hand back, feeling a deep platonic bond between us.

I knew Beatrice would be fine as we finished our late-night drinks and snacks. She had the strength, resilience, and heart to overcome any obstacle. I would be there every step of the way, cheering her on and reminding her of how incredible she was.

Even though we smoothed many things out that evening, I had a disturbing dream that evening. It was a dream that felt all too real, as if I were actually witnessing the chaos and destruction unfolding before my eyes.

AS I GAZED OUT AT THE HORIZON, MY HEART STARTED TO race when I saw the waters of the bay in a frenzy. Wild waves crashed against the shore, violently whipping up and down, causing panic and havoc among the town's residents. People were screaming and running for cover, but there seemed to be nowhere safe to hide.

In the distance, I saw Beatrice standing near the water's edge—her visage twisted in fear and disbelief. Before I could do anything to help her, a massive wave came crashing down, knocking her off her feet and sweeping her out to sea. I felt a rush of helplessness wash over me as I watched the raging waves carry Beatrice away. I tried to scream out to her, to make her hear me above the roar of the storm. But my voice was lost in the din. Petrified, I realized that I was powerless to save her. I could only watch as the sea swallowed her up. Carried far, far away from the shore. Lost to the depths.

CHAPTER EIGHT

THE BIKE RIDE

> *When reason has left one's side before the right time has come, the enduring love one seeks becomes unattainable, seemingly placed upon the highest branch of the tallest tree.*

It was the late fall of our first year of training. Since the pregnancy complications and difficult cesarean delivery Claire had survived, I was back in a mostly normal rhythm of seeing patient after patient in the clinic for annual wellness visits, well-child checkups, and other run-of-the-mill office visits. I was burying my face in a Cobb salad when Vincent suddenly appeared with his classic huge smile plastered on his face. Waving his hands to bring the others over, he proposed emphatically that we should do *"una vuelta de* Frieden Bay."

"We have to do this together," he insisted. "There's so much to see around the area. I want you all to experience the beautiful views I do whenever I bike around town."

He eagerly presented us with the bike route he had mapped out to take us eighteen miles across the major highlights of the town and nearby area. Frieden Bay was known for its charming twin lighthouses, the bustling harbor and docks, dense forests, and colorful streets lined with shops and restaurants. This route would take us past these points of interest and more. Beatrice, Soraya, and I looked at each other. All of us were intrigued by Vincent's proposal and looking forward to exploring the town on our bikes.

"When do you want to do this?" I asked, shoveling a forkful of boiled egg and lettuce into my mouth.

"As soon as possible," Vincent asserted, delighted by our interest in the plan. "Does everyone already have a bicycle, or do we need to rent any? I have a spare bike, but it doesn't have pedal assist, which may be helpful for this ride."

"I will borrow that one as long as nobody else needs it," Soraya spoke up. "I sold my old bicycle before we moved out here."

Vincent wrote a note about Soraya needing his bike before whipping his head around toward Beatrice and me.

"Bea and I are good; we have our electric bikes," I glanced at her, noticing her affirming smile. "I just need to air up my tires before that long of a ride."

The next weekend, Vincent and I met at my apartment first thing in the morning. I had to get creative with storing my bike since there were no metal racks or other ways of keeping a bicycle safe outside, so I opted for keeping it in pieces under my bed. Grabbing the frame and wheels of the electric bike, I checked its battery, making sure it was fully charged. I had invested in this back when I was a medical student, and it had become my preferred mode of transportation overnight. Its sleek design and powerful motor allowed me to effortlessly glide through the heavily trafficked streets of the city I lived in and soak in the various sights and sounds. Unfortunately, the narrow cobblestone roadways and paths of Frieden Bay made daily commutes on my bike tough, so I stuck with driving my trusty sedan and walking when the weather was particularly good.

After reassembling my bike, Vincent helped me carry it toward the parking lot, where I extended the kickstand to let it sit for a while.

"When will the others be here?" I asked, double-checking the tires with my pressure gauge and inserting the battery into its housing on the frame.

"There they are," Vincent indicated, shielding his eyes from the sun with his left hand.

Within a few moments, Beatrice and Soraya wheeled over to us, dressed in complete bicycling outfits. After gathering together and ensuring we had everything we needed for the day, we set out on our alfresco adventure, backpacks loaded with sunscreen, snacks, and water. The sun shone brightly in the clear blue sky, and a gentle breeze carried the always enjoyable scent of the coastal town's many evergreen trees. We followed Vincent as he led us through the winding streets of Frieden Bay, pointing out interesting landmarks and spinning yarns about supposed ghost sightings in the hotels along the shoreline.

We started slowly, reveling in the warm sun overhead. The streets were relatively quiet at this time of day, allowing us to navigate the town easily. Pedaling side by side, we bantered and quipped, giving each other a hard time for our silliest habits. As we continued our journey, we veered off the main roads, opting for quieter paths that led to hidden nooks and crannies of the town. From the trails running along the terraces, we could glimpse the vastness of the sea, extending seemingly infinitely toward the horizon. The crashing waves created a soothing melody that accompanied us as we cycled, especially over the clopping sound of our tires bouncing off the cobblestone. Each time we turned a corner, a new vista captivated us with its pulchritude.

I relished the loveliness of our surroundings. The tall trees lined the paths, providing a natural canopy that shielded us from the day's heat. Red, orange, and yellow leaves blanketed the ground and softened the sound of the rolling rubber. Autumnal flowers of all colors saluted us in their majestic vibrancy along the sides, adding a touch of magic to our journey. Occasionally, we passed by couples walking hand in hand, families enjoying picnics, and children frolicking. It was a reminder that life was meant to be savored and that moments like this were what truly mattered. I felt proud that I was staying true to myself and not losing sight of what kept me whole.

Our first stop was the northern lighthouse, where we climbed to the top and marveled at the astounding views of the town and its aquatic neighbor to the east, snapping photos with our phones. From there, we cycled along the coastline, admiring the deep cerulean color of the bay and the peregrine falcons darting back and forth overhead. We rode along the docks, noting all the boats and ships stationed in the waters. Making a brief stop at the southern lighthouse, we scrambled to the top to capture more photos from the other side of the bay, which revealed the nuanced differences between the two sides that one could only appreciate with a sightseeing tour like this. Returning to our bicycles, Vincent ardently pointed to a small dirt path toward the smaller mountains south of the town. My motor loudly whirred as we cycled up the mountain, destined for the top.

As we reached the summit of Mount Bradford, we parked our bikes and sat on the ground to catch our breath and regain our strength for the second half of *la vuelta*. Vincent started outlining his post-residency goals as we enjoyed a simple lunch of apples, cucumber and cream cheese sandwiches, and peanut butter, all while taking in the views of the valley below. He talked about his hopes to operate a clinic where he could work with patients on lifestyle-focused management of their chronic diseases. He spoke of our challenges in the current healthcare system, wherein insurance coverage was often a barrier to providing comprehensive care to patients.

Vincent lamented the lack of resources and support for preventive care, which was essential to help patients manage their maladies effectively. These troubles weighed heavily on him as he dove into his concerns about not being able to fulfill his dreams in the face of such insurmountable obstacles. Unexpectedly, he then shared his one wish—a simple yet profound wish.

"If I had one wish," Vincent said, his eyes shining with hope, "it would be to make sure every man, woman, and child had access to a bicycle and safe green areas. Without them, we're just going to keep getting sicker and suffer from the burden of human-made disease as we get older."

We listened as Vincent explained his vision of a world where everyone could stay active, connect with nature, and improve their overall health and well-being. He spoke passionately about the transformative power of exercise and fresh air and how he believed that, by providing these simple resources to every individual, we could make a real difference in the fight against chronic diseases. I knew that the scientific literature supported everything he was saying and deplored the fact that we had not already prioritized these strategies as a society.

Vincent's words stayed with us as we finished lunch and prepared to head down the mountain. I was inspired by his vision and passion and was determined to support him in any way possible to make his dream a reality. Following the detour, we continued on our journey, passing through the harbor where fishing boats bobbed in the water and seagulls swooped down in search of scraps. As the sun began to set, we made our way back to where we started, our hearts happy and our faces flushed from the day's adventures. Vincent's idea of *esta vuelta* turned out to be the perfect way to spend a day exploring the charm of our little town with good friends by our side. Although we were tired, we had one more thing to do before retiring.

As the daylight of the evening waned, we found ourselves in the heart of the town. The streets were illuminated with the many lampposts' incandescent light. The town's energy enveloped us as we walked through it. We crossed through the crowded town square, passing by street performers, food stalls, and neon signs. We sat together on the beach and watched the stars twinkle in the sky, pointing out constellations and asterisms far away from the light pollution of our apartment complexes. Our laughter filled the air, a symphony harmonizing with the chilly wind rushing by us. As we hugged each other goodbye, promising to do it all again soon, we were grateful for the simple joys of friendship, adventure, and the beauty of Frieden Bay.

Before heading back into his apartment, Vincent turned to me, satisfaction written on his face.

"Can you believe we biked around the whole town and up a mountain? Makes me feel very accomplished for just one day's work."

"Thank you for organizing this," I said, stretching my upper body. "I needed something like this to break up the monotony of work and lectures."

"I'm glad you had a good time. I mean it when I say we need to do this again. I would love for '*La Vuelta de* Frieden Bay' to become a regular pastime for our program. I know others would get out more if they knew how nice it is to feel the wind on their faces from the bike seat."

"You're right," I concurred. "We'll spread the word and get people engaged. Maybe this could even be a bigger project. Let me sleep on it and get back to you later."

After the particularly stirring conversations with Vincent, I was filled with enthusiasm and renewed conviction about biking, so I kept my electric bicycle in my living room and rode it to the clinic and hospital as often as possible. I appealed to Mr. Haron about installing a bike rack, and in three weeks, we had one installed near the parking lot. Biking transformed from a forgotten pastime into my daily routine in the following weeks. On one frigid Tuesday morning in December, I decided to speak to Vincent. I caught him in the hallway at the clinic, hunched over some disability paperwork.

"Vin," I said to him, trying to get his attention without startling him. "I wanted to follow up on what we talked about after our big bike ride, about taking the biking efforts to the community."

He looked up, eyes lighting with the kind of fervor he exuded the day of our group ride.

"I remember you saying that. How would we go about doing this?"

"We could write an op-ed," I suggested. "We could present your vision to the entire town in *The Frieden Phoenix*, not just the patients who come here."

Vincent's toothy smile was all the encouragement I needed.

Over the next three days, Vincent and I huddled over our espressos in The Nook after our clinic shifts, brainstorming and typing vigorously. Our combined perspectives on this issue came together into a convincing argument for why every resident—young and old—should consider bicycling and how local policymakers could pave the way for a more physically active Frieden Bay. We detailed the improved traffic conditions, health benefits, and even the possible economic uplift for local businesses from increased bike traffic through the town. To our delight, the local newspaper, *The Frieden Phoenix*, published the op-ed the following Sunday. It was met with surprising zest. Feedback poured in through emails, social media, and even word of mouth from patients in the clinic.

The community's response was overwhelmingly in favor of exploring this idea further, which served as the impetus for Mayor Judy Harrison to invite Vincent and me to her office to discuss implementing a sustainable biking program in Frieden Bay. We formally laid out our proposal in the oak-paneled conference room at Town Hall with a circle of interested council members around us.

"The cornerstone of this initiative," Vincent stated confidently, "would be a voucher program that subsidizes the purchase of new bicycles and safety gear like helmets. Financial incentives would undoubtedly increase participation."

Mayor Harrison nodded, scribbling notes onto a large memo pad.

"And what would be the plan for ongoing community engagement? Would my people need to be involved in that in any particular way?"

"That part would be simple," I chimed in, suddenly brave in Vincent's presence. "We would organize a community-wide bike ride. Imagine a 'Discover Frieden Bay on Two Wheels' day, where families can explore routes, local businesses can set up booths, and we can collectively enjoy the outdoors."

It was a vision that everyone in the room could get behind. Excitement buzzed through the air as details and plans began to form. Before the meeting concluded, the mayor confirmed the council's enthusiasm for our ideas and green-lit the initiative. Weeks later, the inaugural 'Discover Frieden Bay on Two Wheels' day was a spectacle of colors and shiny bicycles. Residents of all ages mounted bikes of all sizes—some shaky and unsure, others confident and swift. Vincent and I rode side by side for most of the event, marveling at what had begun as a simple conversation in a clinic hallway and had transformed into a community movement.

As we rode past the newly installed bike lane signs and refurbished bike racks, Vincent leaned over to me.

"Sometimes all it takes is a little push, huh?"

"Yep," I replied, feeling the cool wind against my face. "A little push and a willingness to ride the distance. It looks like we're making your dream a reality little by little. I guess it's the perk of working in a small town."

A COUPLE OF WEEKS LATER, VINCENT, SORAYA, AND I were dining on asparagus, rosemary mashed potatoes, and baked chicken at my apartment. Beatrice was scheduled for a call shift at the hospital to admit patients from the emergency department, so we had to make the most of being the three amigos without our fourth.

"I still cannot believe that Mayor Harrison called you all over and got behind the community biking initiative," Soraya said, slicing off a piece of chicken with her knife. "You all are the poster children for getting things done; it's so inspiring."

"You were the one who made this all possible," Vincent remarked, pointing his fork at me. "You helped me distill down my passion for this stuff into a form that garnered the mayor's attention, and for that, I'm grateful."

As everyone finished their food, I cleared away our plates and silverware, placing everything neatly into the sink and opening the freezer to pull out the bourbon ice cream I purchased for dessert.

"You know, I had another idea if you guys were interested in discussing it," I mentioned coyly.

"Spill it, brother," Vincent demanded, turning around in his chair to face me. "Chances are good that it'll be another winner."

After preparing and serving three bowls of ice cream, I sat down with my two co-residents, and together, we cooked up another promising project: "Walk & Talk," a chance for the townsfolk to engage in walks with local healthcare professionals. It was designed not just for being physically active together but also as a platform for denizens to discuss health-related matters informally, seeking advice while strolling through Frieden Bay.

"Think about it," I said, hands animatedly sketching the vision in the air. "It's not just about walking; it's about learning, communicating, and building a healthier community. We could change lives with this and capitalize on the new interest in getting outside."

From the lively looks on their faces, I could tell that Vincent and Soraya were convinced. So, after filling in Beatrice on the plan over a lunch of pepperoni pizza the next day, we began our mission. Armed with bundles of bright yellow flyers and endless enthusiasm that evening, we spread the word. Every lamppost, community bulletin board, and local business window in Frieden Bay soon sported announcements of the inaugural "Walk & Talk" session. Soraya set up event pages online, while Beatrice appealed to people visiting the community center to attract the older members of the population. The community response was heartwarming, with an outpouring of interest that exceeded even the success of the biking initiative.

The first "Walk & Talk" was set on a breezy Saturday morning. The rendezvous point was in Dolphin Park, under an old red maple that had witnessed countless picnics. As the clock struck nine, dozens of community members from all walks of life congregated, including resident physicians from other specialties. Some were geared in sporty attire, while others were in comfortable casual clothes. Deeply impressed with our community involvement, Dr. Altamura offered to help us in any way possible. Carefully considering the role he could play, we collectively decided to have him be our speaker to kick off the first community walk.

Standing in the middle of the crowd, Dr. Altamura delivered a brief but powerful speech about the benefits of regular walking and how it could be seamlessly integrated into daily routines. He was engaging and informative, dispelling myths and encouraging questions.

"As doctors, we often see the outcome of neglect more than prevention. Let's change that narrative starting today, right here in Frieden Bay," he proclaimed, beaming at the crowd that nodded and applauded in agreement.

The group was divided into smaller clusters, each accompanied by a healthcare professional. I found myself walking with a group led by Dr. Mose, who was answering a flurry of questions from curious parents. Soraya walked alongside, live-streaming parts of the walk to social media to further promote the initiative. As we walked along the scenic trails, conversations flowed effortlessly. Topics ranged from managing diabetes to the benefits of mindfulness in daily living to how much dirt is safe for a child to eat. The relaxed setting made it easy for everyone to talk openly, ask questions, and share personal anecdotes. By the time we circled back to the red maple tree, the group was alive with new connections and plans for future walks. People lingered, not just to chat, but to thank us for organizing the event.

As Vincent and I watched everyone gradually disperse, we felt accomplished.

"Who knew," Vincent mused, a satisfied grin splitting his face, "that all it took was a few steps to bring us all closer together?"

With the undeniable success of that first morning, "Walk & Talk" became a staple in Frieden Bay's calendar. Each walk strengthened the fabric of our community, weaving closer ties and nurturing a collective commitment toward health and happiness. Even though Vincent and I made strides toward wellness in Frieden Bay, something dark inside my mind reviled me. *How long would they stay active when this was probably just a fad?* I never said a word about this to Vincent, choosing instead to control these negative thoughts on my own.

CHAPTER NINE

Guidance Faltered That Day

> *Those embracing the empty lights of a painted heaven try as they might to scale the tree, finding that brute force alone leaves them where they began.*

It was a dreary summer day in late July, which marked the beginning of my second year of residency training. Drizzling rain covered my nylon jacket, and dense, black clouds obstructed any hint of daylight in the small town. In the distance, a monstrous thunderstorm brewed over the Frieden Sea. Intense flashes of lightning tore through the sky, with its subsequent thunder shaking everything along the shoreline. With my trusty electric bike at a local shop for repairs, I decided to risk the walk back home. Fearsome gales ripped across my path, sending a chill across my skin and nearly knocking me to the ground more than once.

Keeping my head down to avoid the blinding force of the winds, I visualized my to-do list for this evening, including the emails I would need to send and the patient portal messages I would need to answer. I looked at the cracks and uneven portions of the sidewalk, occasionally peering up to make sure I was not unwittingly on a collision course with someone else. As the rain picked up in intensity, my pace quickened to avoid getting any more drenched than I already was.

Out of the corner of my eye, an unexpected flurry of hands caught my attention. Unaware of what was occurring, I changed course and sprinted to the beach's railing.

"Please, come here! We need help!" a deep, gravelly voice called from the dim beach below.

I hurriedly located the nearest staircase and surefootedly descended to the wet sands. As I rapidly approached the two people who had waved me down, I noticed another person sprawled out supine on the ground with torn and soiled clothing.

"What's going on?" I loudly called back before reaching the small group. "What's the situation?"

"There was an accident. I think this man was out on the water before the storm blew in from the south," a hooded man with a similar but slightly higher-pitched voice replied.

"Oh, no..." I gasped, staring blankly at the man.

It was Dr. Altamura. Every droplet of blood drained from my face in a flash. My gut caved in on itself. I was paralyzed, only able to use my levator palpebrae superioris muscles to keep my eyes open.

"Do you know this guy or something?" the deep-voiced man asked, clearly noticing my motionlessness.

I ignored the question and wrenched my muscles out of their dormancy before sprinting to Dr. Altamura's side. His respirations were shallow, and he was severely injured. His clothing was ripped to shreds in parts, which exposed weeping wounds along his extremities and abdomen. As I examined him more closely, I noticed his weak chest excursion, gross deformity of the right tibia and femur, and generalized pale skin. I touched him and felt that he was likely hypothermic from the exposure to the elements and seawater.

"Should we move him under that pier over there?" the first man suggested, pointing to a sheltered spot a few yards away.

"No, we can't be sure his cervical spine is stable," I quickly answered. "Is an ambulance on the way?"

"Yes, we called EMS as soon as we found him," the second person replied. "It looked like he washed up on the shore. We haven't seen any sign of debris from a boat, but that's the only thing we figure could have happened."

"Dr. Altamura!" I yelled, kneeling beside him. "Dr. Altamura, if you can hear me, squeeze my fingers."

No response. I placed my fingers on his neck to check his central pulse. It was thready, but it was there. Continuing my focused evaluation, I palpated his lower extremities and felt clear segments of lift-off along his anterior right tibia and femur. I also felt crepitus along the lateral aspect of his right fifth through seventh ribs, which made me worry about possible hemothorax from the likely underlying rib fractures.

"He's still alive," I said, relieved. "We need to keep him stable and as warm and dry as possible until EMS arrives."

The three of us worked quickly, using our jackets to cover him and protect him from the rain. I did not have anything to make a splint out of for his right lower extremity, but the paramedics would be able to assist soon. Within a few moments, we had two other people over to provide help, and one younger woman was able to supply us with beach towels that we used to dry off Dr. Altamura.

After several minutes, our efforts were rewarded: Dr. Altamura grunted and opened his eyes weakly. He was completely disoriented and unintelligible when he tried to speak. We kept talking to him, urging him to stay awake and hold on. Minutes stretched into what felt like hours as we waited for help. The rain soaked through our clothes, making us shiver from the cold. But none of us cared; we were preoccupied with keeping Dr. Altamura alive by any means possible.

Finally, the sound of sirens pierced through the howling wind and rain. The paramedics arrived with their equipment and rushed to Dr. Altamura's side.

"We found him unconscious on the beach," I explained to the paramedics. "He was breathing slowly, but I could feel a pulse. We focused on keeping him still, warm, and dry until you all got here."

The paramedics worked efficiently, attaching monitors to Dr. Altamura's chest and finger, administering oxygen, stabilizing his cervical spine with a rigid collar, and applying a temporary splint to his right leg.

They carefully loaded Dr. Altamura onto a stretcher and carried him to the waiting ambulance. I watched as they drove away, hoping that he would make it through this accident. After they left, the two men who had called for help thanked me for stopping and assisting. They introduced themselves as Liam and Jonathan, two local brothers and construction workers who had been heading home when they stumbled upon Dr. Altamura on the beach.

"You really were a hero today," Liam stated, his eyes filled with gratitude. "My brother and I know CPR and the basics, but clearly, you are trained in this stuff. You in the medical field?"

"Yes," I replied, deeply appreciative of the kind words. "I work at Alta Vista. Dr. Altamura is one of our teaching doctors and my mentor. He has saved countless lives in this town. It was the least I could do to try and help him."

"I can't believe you know this guy," Jonathan declared, shaking his head in disbelief. "Saving someone you know... That must've been a hard thing to do."

"More than you can imagine," I confessed, rubbing my sore forearms.

We stood there for a brief moment, soaked to the bone but feeling a bond of camaraderie that had been formed under the most unexpected circumstances. After coexisting in that space and time, I left, intending to return to my apartment to get clean and dry. My muscles started to ache from my dropping body temperature, so I knew the safest thing to do was head to

Beatrice's apartment to get a ride back to mine for a shower and a change of clothes.

I jogged to the complex and hurried up the stairs to her unit, taking shelter under the covered section before getting to her door. Having noticed her car on the way over, I had a good feeling she was in for the afternoon. I knocked vigorously on the door, and Beatrice opened it almost instantly, still dressed in blue scrubs from her day at work.

"What're you doing here? Did something happen?" she interrogated, observing my dripping and dirty clothes.

"Yes," I answered, teeth chattering behind my lips. "Do you mind if I dry off for a second? I need to tell you something."

Without another word, Beatrice hurried off to gather a couple of large towels from her bathroom and then handed them to me.

"Dr. Altamura was in an accident," I explained, drying myself with one of the towels. "He's pretty badly injured and on his way to the hospital."

"How did this happen?" Beatrice gasped, placing her hand over her mouth.

"I ran into two guys who found him first," I said, drying my hair and face. "They found him washed up on the beach. They think he was out at sea on his boat before something took it down."

"Oh my God!" Beatrice exclaimed, rubbing her cheek. "It must've been the tropical storm. I was reading about it on my weather app. I wonder if he was caught off guard while he was cruising."

I wrung out my shirt to the best of my ability before using the second towel to absorb as much water as possible from my clothes.

"That has to be right; this weather's crazy. I'm so sorry to bother you, but I needed some help after getting caught up with responding to the scene. Can you drive me back to my apartment so I can get cleaned up and put on some dry clothes?"

Beatrice forced a consternated smile and nodded. She ran back inside to get her raincoat, wallet, keys, and two more large towels before we moved back downstairs to her car. After setting the towels up on the leather upholstery of the passenger seat and floorboard, I climbed inside and sighed in relief as the seat warmer and hot air from the car's vents soothed my tired body after a few minutes.

"I can't believe this happened to him." Beatrice shook her head as she drove us across town to where I lived. "It's inconceivable that someone as experienced as he is on the waters could end up in a situation like this."

"I know what you mean," I responded with my head leaned back and eyes closed. "Sometimes, terrible things happen to good people with good intentions and capabilities. Maybe he just made a mistake and forgot to check the forecast before heading out. Regardless, I just hope he's okay. It looked like he had two open fractures: one along his tibia and another along his femur. I didn't want to alarm the men I was with since they aren't in healthcare, but his right leg looked horrible."

Beatrice gasped upon hearing the description of his injuries. We pulled into my complex, and I invited Beatrice inside to have a cup of tea while I tended to what I needed. I kicked off my muck-covered tennis shoes before entering the unit and closed the door behind the two of us. After showering thoroughly and changing into dry clothes, I plopped down beside Beatrice on the couch, where she drank some herbal tea and watched the weather report on the local news station. The meteorologist provided an update on the tropical storm lingering over the area due to a low-pressure system that moved in earlier in the day.

"Do you want to go see him?" I asked, putting on my back-up pair of tennis shoes and tying them. "I bet they have him over in the trauma bay by now. I can drive us since you were kind enough to get me back here."

Together, Beatrice and I ventured back out into the steady rain, and I drove over to the hospital's main entrance to avoid the chaos around the entrance to the emergency department. Using our badges, we accessed a stairwell for employees from the lobby to the nurse's station. After weaving through a series of labyrinthine corridors, we made our way to the emergency department and checked in with the charge nurse, who directed us to a bed on the farthest end of the trauma bay. My heart raced as I pictured Dr. Altamura's mangled body lying on the bed. The image of him being rushed over here in the ambulance earlier was still fresh in my mind.

We calmly walked down to his bed, where the pale blue curtains had been drawn around him. I breathed slowly and deeply as soon as the faint outline of Dr. Altamura entered my vision from behind the thin curtain. As we opened the curtain, we saw that he was resting his eyes, a nasal cannula firmly positioned under his nose. I could hear the steady beeping of the cardiac monitor filling the silence of the bay.

My eyes darted around the makeshift room, taking in the various medical equipment and supplies. Stable vital signs on the monitor. A mostly empty bag of packed red blood cells and Ringer's lactate solution hanging from the IV pole. The telltale plastic of a chest tube emerging from the right side of his chest for that traumatic hemothorax I had suspected back on the beach. The raised sheets likely concealed the splint on his right leg, remaining in place until orthopedic surgery could evaluate him.

Beatrice and I slowly approached his bedside—our footsteps muffled on the cold linoleum floor. We sat down in nearby chairs, our hearts on tenterhooks. Dr. Altamura had been a great mentor, friend, and inspiration to me, and I knew that Beatrice also looked up to him. Seeing him lying here struck a deep chord within me.

Beatrice reached out and gently brushed a strand of hair away from his forehead. She said his skin felt cool to the touch, which gave me a flashback to touching his cold skin on the beach. I observed the lines etched across his face, the wrinkles that had deepened with each passing year. Each wrinkle contained a story: his years spent struggling with operating boats until he finally mastered it; his work at an urban free clinic when he was studying medicine in Boston; his grand speeches on common dermatologic conditions at annual conferences; his years of patient, compassionate teaching.

As we sat there for what felt like an eternity, my mind drifted back to cruising out onto the Frieden Sea with him one year ago. I could still feel the warm wooden deck beneath my feet. Dr. Altamura had invited us to join him for a day of mindfulness and connection before our schedules became hectic. We talked, laughed, and enjoyed life's simple pleasures that day. Because of him, our cohort had become close very quickly, with us being almost inseparable now.

I thought about our unforgettable hike up to the overlook, the many evenings spent discussing art and philosophy in The Beacon, our private conversations in the clinic and hospital about side projects we were working on, and our safe and supportive debriefs after difficult patient cases. On top of the countless patients he had made a positive impact on, he made living a well-lived life look easy. He had been more than just a physician; he symbolized hope, compassion, and unwavering dedication to his community.

"Hey, you two," Dr. Altamura muttered, turning his head to face us. "It's sure great to see you. Do you all know how I got here?"

With a burst of happiness, Beatrice got up and wrapped her arms around Dr. Altamura's neck.

"Two Good Samaritans and I found you on the beach," I answered, standing up and stepping right next to him and Beatrice. "Were you out on your boat earlier?"

Dr. Altamura closed his eyes, trying very hard to remember what had taken place before he fell unconscious. He was out on the Frieden Sea when he saw some distant storm clouds accumulating to the south. He was so far out that he could not get back to shore before the tempest was upon him. Rogue waves crashed into *The Albatross* and swept him off course. The winds and waves were too strong, and he was thrown into the churning water as the whole boat capsized. Everything went dark when a large piece of wood struck him in his chest.

Tears welled up in our eyes as we listened to Dr. Altamura's recount.

"I'm just glad you're alive," Beatrice verbalized, putting out what we were all thinking. "It's miraculous."

As the day wore on and the rain finally stopped, the quiet hum of the hospital seemed to envelop us. We sat there, perfectly still, knowing this was just the beginning of a long journey. The road to recovery would be challenging, but with Dr. Altamura's resilience and the unwavering support of those who loved him, I believed in his ability to regain his health.

"Knock, knock," we heard someone announce from the other side of the encircling curtain. "It's Dr. Winston with ortho coming in."

A burly man standing about six feet tall sauntered in, his long brown hair bouncing in a ponytail.

"It's good to see you all," he waved at Beatrice and me, his mollifying presence a welcome change of pace. "Virgil, I made arrangements to get you back to the OR tonight so we can start working on your right leg. Based on your imaging, we have at least three separate surgeries ahead of us. Are you okay with going back right now?"

"Let's do it, Louis," Dr. Altamura grinned, shaking Dr. Winston's large hand. "I'll catch up with you all again very soon."

As Beatrice and I vacated Dr. Altamura's makeshift room to give the orthopedics team some space to transport him back for his first surgery, I reached out and held Dr. Altamura's hand, my grip firm yet gentle.

"Dr. Altamura," I whispered, my voice barely audible. "You're strong, and you have so much more to give to this world."

Dr. Altamura was admitted to the hospital on Friday, the same day I found him down on the beach. That weekend, I visited him daily to see how he was doing. Dr. Winston pulled many strings to expedite the reconstructive and direct fracture repair surgeries Dr. Altamura needed. While it was hard on his body, Dr. Altamura remained in good spirits, optimistic about his prognosis and future recovery in the inpatient rehabilitation unit. When I left on Sunday evening, I could see his progress and felt reassured.

I returned to the clinic on Monday, ready to get back into a normal rhythm for the week. While reviewing my patients' charts in preparation for my morning session, I heard the familiar thumping sound of polished patent leather shoes approaching.

"Good morning," Dr. Calisto's voice carried across the workroom.

I sat up sharply and turned toward his voice.

"Before starting your clinic today, would you mind chatting with me briefly about something?" Dr. Calisto requested in an uncharacteristically bland manner.

I rose from my chair and followed Dr. Calisto over to his office. My mind raced with what he needed to say to me that was inappropriate for the workroom. As we entered his office and he closed the door behind us, I hesitantly lowered myself into one of the two tawny leather chairs in front of his desk.

"I appreciate you coming with me. I have to tell you something before announcing it to the other residents and faculty," he started as he settled into his black office chair. "Have you received any recent updates about Dr. Altamura?"

My eyes narrowed as the gears started spinning faster and faster to anticipate what he was about to tell me.

"I saw him yesterday evening, and he was making progress with physical therapy after his third surgery."

Dr. Calisto's eerily stoic face provided hints at something dark on the horizon.

"He was," he proceeded, stopping to regroup before pressing ahead. "I need to give you an update on that."

Mounting dread cemented in my abdomen as I realized something was amiss.

"Dr. Altamura passed away last night."

The muscles in my legs tensed so hard that my chair moved backward by several inches. I sat in nonplussed silence for several moments, unable to grasp what Dr. Calisto just said to me.

"Wh-what do you mean? I don't understand," I stammered, visibly shaking. "I just saw him. He was fine."

"I don't have all of the details," Dr. Calisto responded in a hushed tone. "I was told he had a complication related to his surgeries. It sounded like a venous thromboembolic complication, probably a massive pulmonary embolism."

I jumped out of my chair and walked over to the window, hyperventilating as if I had just finished running a marathon.

"Dr. C-Calisto... How could this happen to him?"

Dr. Calisto rose from his seat and shuffled over to my side, wrapping his arm around my shoulders to console me.

"I can only imagine what you're going through right now. He was your mentor, and I know how close you two were. I'm mourning the loss of him as a dear friend I have known for many years. He was a figure larger than life, not only here in Frieden Bay but throughout the nation."

After discussing the disturbing news in more detail, Dr. Calisto insisted that I take the rest of the day off to attend to my grieving and be with loved ones. He told me he would see my patients today. I drove home in complete silence, too sorrowful to enjoy a song or podcast. When I arrived back at the apartment complex, I decided to sit on a bench to practice my deep breathing before going inside. I closed my eyes and focused entirely on the contraction and expansion of my abdomen as I could hear Dr. Altamura's words of wisdom echoing in my mind.

"It's good to see you again," a familiar voice called out. "How are you doing?"

Charles Haron trotted down the terraced pathway leading toward me from the complex's main office. Without words, he requested my permission to sit beside me on the bench, which I gave him.

"I am very sorry about what happened to Dr. Altamura," Mr. Haron said gently after observing a moment of silence as he sat beside me. "I learned what happened to him last night from a close friend. He was a good man and a dear friend to many of us. He was my primary care physician for many years, and I admired his compassion and attention in taking care of me. He will be missed, never to be forgotten."

With a largely expressionless face, I slowly turned toward the landlord.

"Thank you, Mr. Haron. I appreciate your kind words about him."

"I imagine that it must be hard for you right now, and that is exactly why I want to make sure that you know that you can come to any of us here in the community whenever you need reassurance and support. We are here for you and would do anything to help you, especially during this difficult time."

I smiled weakly at him.

"Thank you again."

I DASHED THROUGH THE DOUBLE DOORS OF ALTA VISTA Hospital's front entrance, nearly toppling over a display holding pamphlets about local transportation services. Despite not being anywhere near it, I could sense something was amiss in Dr. Altamura's room on the third floor. In a flurry of motion, I hurtled toward the elevators, frantically pushing at the "Up" button before hastily abandoning that option to climb the stairs as fast as my feet would allow me.

Completely winded, I burst through the door from the stairwell to the third-floor surgical-medical wards to run to the window of Room #329. Although I was standing outside the room, I could clearly hear everything inside. A nurse stood at the bedside, administering hydromorphone through the peripheral intravenous line. Dr. Altamura was lying there, soundly sleeping. His vital signs, including his oxygen saturation level, were within normal limits.

As the nurse turned away to exit the room, Dr. Altamura's eyes instantly shot open, revealing a grimace before he gripped the center of his chest.

"I need... I need help," he forced out before coughing up a large amount of bright red blood. "Something's wrong."

Gross hemoptysis. This must be the pulmonary embolism, I thought, pressing my hands up against the glass in horror. *You have to help him.*

Terror in her expression, the nurse scrambled to the wall nearest her to activate the rapid-response protocol. She hurried to the doorway and called for all available nursing staff to respond immediately. Dr. Altamura continued coughing up blood while his heart rate and respiratory rate spiked and his oxygen saturation level plummeted, leaving him acutely hypoxemic.

Please, don't let him die, I thought, unable to vocalize anything.

The on-site internist raced into the room, quickly examined Dr. Altamura, and then shouted for systemic thrombolytic therapy and an additional peripheral line for unfractionated heparin. The charge nurse hastily pushed the crash cart into the room. Another nurse drew up the bolus dose of tissue plasminogen activator to break up the clot obstructing his pulmonary vessels. Yet another nurse came down the hallway with a pharmacist in tow, carrying the heparin to begin his anticoagulation.

I attempted to join in on the emergency interventions, but no matter how much I tried to move, my feet were stuck firmly to the floor. Incapable of contributing, I helplessly stood there, wailing as I watched my mentor *in extremis*. No matter what the team did—non-rebreather mask, thrombolysis, anticoagulation—Dr. Altamura's condition continued to deteriorate.

Then, I saw the fatal sequence: sustained monomorphic ventricular tachycardia followed by ventricular fibrillation. I covered my eyes and screamed, but no sound came out. With all sounds now muffled, I looked on in horror as the physician called for defibrillation and as the others on the team started chest compressions and prepared epinephrine after finding no pulse. Shock after shock, the ventricular fibrillation persisted. Eventually, the dreaded final arrhythmia occurred: asystole.

I buried my head in my hands, unable to watch more of this. I felt a strange suction from behind me, and as I turned my head to see what was happening, an enormous dark portal appeared, consuming everything in its vicinity. Within only a few moments, I was viciously ripped away and pulled into the portal. Before the darkness consumed me, I looked back one last time at Dr. Altamura, who lay lifeless on the bed as the responding medical team ended the resuscitation attempt.

CHAPTER TEN

The Scent of Coffee

> *The mind of the fool takes flight, and it feels that so, too, must its body since love lies above it—out of reach and nearly out of sight.*

Losing Dr. Altamura was one of the most painful experiences of my life, and what made it worse was not being able to attend his funeral. Since most of his family was in Connecticut, they decided to have his funeral service near Bridgeport instead of in Frieden Bay. I sent a beautiful floral arrangement to the address his siblings provided and sat alone in my apartment, remembering him and wordlessly celebrating the extraordinary life he led.

The day after discovering his terrible fate, my co-residents and I gathered near a ship resembling *The Albatross*, unoccupied and floating listlessly in the harbor, to observe the life of a man larger than life in silence. Navigating my grief required taking my responsibilities day by day, focusing on the small things that proved how much of a positive impact he had on me. Fortunately, I had the pleasant distractions of work and spending time with my friends and co-residents. While sitting in the Primary Care Center with Beatrice one morning, her zest for life pulled me away from my troubling thoughts for a short while.

"You've got to check this out," Beatrice announced, pecking at her keyboard. "I'm emailing it to you now."

Chuckling, I clicked on the new message and opened a digital flier for the "Council of Graduate Medical Trainees." The premise was intriguing; this national organization was founded in the 1990s to foster a culture of collaboration among resident and fellow physicians and promote the unionization of medical trainees at participating residency and fellowship programs nationwide. The website listed a number of interesting leadership positions for residents and fellows to take on more active roles in setting institutional priorities and negotiating with local hospital and healthcare system leaders.

"Wow, I've never seen "Beatrice Portinari" written in such huge letters across anything before!" I half-joked with her. "In all seriousness, Bea, you should apply for East Region President. That role would be perfect for you."

Beatrice looked away coyly, baiting me to ask her the natural follow-up question.

"Let me guess. You've already applied, haven't you?"

"I'm one of the finalists under consideration by the Board of Directors for the position," she said in a hushed but exuberant tone. "I would love to do it."

"You've got this, President Dr. Portinari," I told her, jocularly saluting her from my chair.

Two days later, the results came in, and Beatrice bounded through the door leading to the resident workroom that morning to show us something, victory evident in her gestures.

"I've got big news for you all," she started, unable to contain her excitement. "I was selected to serve as this year's Regional President."

Vincent, Soraya, several other residents, and I applauded her at this announcement. This was an excellent opportunity for our program to be involved in organized medicine and collective bargaining for things that would improve the working conditions for resident physicians now and later. There was no better person for this role than Beatrice.

Three months had elapsed since Beatrice was named East Region President in August. During that time, the union gained momentum, and its membership steadily grew to several dozen strong. Under the strong leadership of Beatrice, the union had established several advocacy priorities: fair wages based on national benchmarks, safer working conditions, and improved patient care within the hospital. With her cleverness and fiery determination, Beatrice had spent countless hours rallying her colleagues and organizing meetings to discuss their concerns and propose viable solutions. The union members, all dedicated residents across different medical specialties, stood united in their mission to make a difference in their workplace and create a better environment for themselves and their patients.

On a dismal day in November, Dr. Mose informed us of a tragedy that had befallen the general surgery residency program at Alta Vista. Late in the evening, Leslie Newman, one of the second-year residents, was leaving the hospital after a thirty-two-hour shift because she had to cover for a colleague who had suddenly fallen ill. Enervated and slow to react, Leslie was driving across a bridge when she fell asleep behind the wheel and careened into the guardrail. Her vehicle broke through the guardrail and landed upside down in the waters below, resulting in her death from drowning.

The residents in the various specialties represented in the union demanded a meeting to discuss this appalling situation and devise a plan for negotiations with the Alta Vista CEO to protect residents from endangering themselves and others by creating designated sleep spaces for fatigued workers in the hospital and implementing other risk-mitigation measures. Apparently, Leslie had tried to stay at the hospital to sleep in one of the call rooms, but the few that did exist there were all occupied that evening. When Beatrice learned of this request for a meeting, she polled the resident members for their availability and then scheduled a virtual meeting. She was disturbed by what happened to Leslie and motivated to change things.

I joined Beatrice before the meeting on a chilly Saturday morning to test the teleconferencing platform and make sure everything was in order before she started admitting the attendees. As the hour approached, residents specializing in family medicine, pediatrics, internal medicine, general surgery, emergency medicine, psychiatry, and radiology logged into the virtual meeting. The screen filled with faces—some weary from night shifts, others fueled by the caffeine of their morning coffee.

"Welcome, everyone," Beatrice said, the gravity of the occasion evident in her tone. "Today marks a pivotal step for all of us. This is about sharing our challenges, framing our realities into words, and banding together to carve out solutions. We're here to make Frieden Bay a stepping stone in our careers and a safe and supportive place where we can thrive as professionals and individuals. For this meeting, we'll start with department-specific discussions before coming back together and talking about Leslie Newman and the larger issues we need to broach as a group."

The agenda was simple yet ambitious: the attendees would break into small groups by medical specialty, identify critical issues in their departments, and reconvene to form a unified list of concerns and suggestions. The screen split as they ventured into breakout rooms. In the pediatrics group, the residents voiced concerns about the outsized patient-to-nurse ratios during night shifts, which often left them scrambling and increased the risks of errors. Meanwhile, the general surgery residents, led by a rather outspoken Ahmad Hassan, discussed the relentless nature of their on-call schedules, which barely left room for recovery, let alone personal life. The general surgery residents also closely examined the circumstances that led to Leslie's death.

Back in the internal medicine camp, a soft-spoken Demetrius Jonas mentioned something that resonated with many:

"The lack of timely access to mental health support for residents is alarming. We deal with life and death every day. Our mental well-being isn't just necessary; it's essential for safe patient care." As each subgroup unearthed its particular challenges, the psychiatry residents, including Emily Forsyth, highlighted the inconsistent availability of supervision that often left them feeling isolated in their clinical decisions. This sentiment was surprisingly widespread among the other departments. Haoyu Zhang from radiology raised an issue about outdated equipment that not only slowed them down but potentially compromised diagnostic accuracy. His concerns, backed by eerily similar experiences from others, added to the broadening scope of the discussions.

When the large group reconvened, the screen buzzed with heightened energy as residents reported their findings. The common threads were unmistakable: work-life imbalance, mental health neglect, inadequate supervision, and resource constraints. Skillfully moderating the rapidly unfolding discourse, Beatrice suggested forming a collective document outlining these key issues and proposed reforms. When the time was right, Beatrice brought up the matter of Leslie Newman and made several concrete suggestions about preventing something like this from occurring again. She outlined the demands for dedicated sleep rooms beyond just the call rooms, twenty-four-hour transportation services to prevent impaired driving, and more scheduling oversight to avoid employees working excessively long shifts that do not comply with accreditation standards. Nods pervaded the digital gathering as each resident felt the surge of solidarity—they were not lone voices anymore but a chorus demanding a change.

"Let's compile our recommendations and schedule a meeting with the hospital administration," Beatrice proposed. "We need structured, regular dialogue with them, not just emergency meetings when things boil over."

The agreement was unanimous. The residents concluded their initial meeting with responsibilities assigned to flesh out their proposals further. There was a palpable sense of achievement and purpose amongst them—a first but significant step toward transforming their work lives. As the virtual meeting room emptied, Beatrice sat back and allowed herself a rare moment of quiet satisfaction. From the flickering screen, the waves of positive change seemed almost tangible, and, for the first time in months, the path forward looked a little brighter for the residents of Frieden Bay.

After weeks of hard work and perseverance, Beatrice decided to take the union's demands directly to the hospital's senior leadership. She drafted a carefully worded email to the CEO requesting a meeting to discuss their concerns and present their proposals for collective bargaining. The stakes were high, and Beatrice knew the road ahead would be challenging, but she was determined to see it through. I sat with her in the clinic when she received the response, which signaled the agreement of the CEO to meet and have a comprehensive discussion about the union's most recent meeting. She disclosed that she was cautiously optimistic about this meeting and hoped to persuade the CEO to adopt the union's point of view on the most pressing issues.

When the meeting day arrived, my co-residents, a group of other union representatives, and I made our way to the CEO's office, all dressed professionally. Upon entering the office, we shook hands with the CEO and his assistant and made customary small talk. As we sat down to discuss our concerns, it became abundantly clear that the CEO was hesitant about our requests for collective bargaining. This was the first time in the health system's history that healthcare workers had unionized.

"So, I reviewed your email," the CEO began. "But, could you summarize exactly what you are asking for?"

"Gladly," Beatrice replied, her voice firm. "As the East Region President of our medical trainee union, I have collected feedback from our members, and they unequivocally outlined several key issues: work-life imbalance, mental health neglect, inadequate supervision, and resource constraints. We also have suggestions about preventing tragedies like the one that happened to Dr. Leslie Newman."

"Hmmmm..." the CEO vocalized, emoting minimally. "I offer my condolences to you all and Dr. Newman's family for her tragic death. Can you be more specific about your suggestions?"

In my recent conversations with her, Beatrice and I discussed the damaging trends in corporatized healthcare and the dangers of profits becoming more important than patients. She shared how she had witnessed discrimination, mistreatment of employees, and unfair wages since she started at Alta Vista. She knew that something needed to change and wanted to be a part of that change. In her eyes, I could tell that Beatrice knew she had an uphill battle ahead of her. According to other employees at the hospital and clinic, this CEO was not always receptive to workers' demands. Beatrice had to tread carefully if she wanted to make a difference. She was committed to fighting for what was right, even if it meant going up against the most influential people in the organization.

As we sat across from the CEO, we could feel the tension in the air. We knew this meeting would be a crucial turning point in our negotiations.

"I understand your concerns about the union's demands," Beatrice said calmly. "But we believe these changes are necessary for the well-being of our resident physicians and the larger healthcare team in the hospital and clinics."

The CEO nodded, his expression unreadable.

"I appreciate your passion, Dr. Portinari. However, you must understand that these changes are not easy to implement. As you know, we're breaking ground on a new outpatient infusion center, and we must be good stewards of our community's resources."

I could sense Beatrice's anger rising, but she forced herself to stay calm for the sake of the negotiations.

"I understand that change can be difficult and that our resources are not infinite. I urge you to listen to these concerns. We are the ones who keep the hospital and outpatient clinics running, and we deserve to be treated with respect and fairness."

The CEO sighed and leaned back in his chair, shooting a wry smile at his assistant.

"I hear what you're saying, Dr. Portinari. I will take your concerns into consideration. But please understand that there are limits to what we can do. It may have to be one small step this year and another the year after."

Beatrice nodded suspiciously, her determination still burning bright.

"I understand, but we will not stop fighting for what's right. We can create a better workplace for everyone."

As we left the meeting, we knew the road ahead would be turbulent and fraught with potential setbacks and pitfalls. No matter how we looked at it, this fight for better working conditions and fair treatment would not be easy, but Beatrice was ready to take on the challenge. Despite our disappointment in the CEO's responses today, Beatrice and the union members refused to back down.

Beatrice paced back and forth at my apartment, a frown etching deeper into her forehead by the minute. I sat at my dining room table, watching her and taking notes about what we were mulling together. It was the day after the unproductive meeting with the CEO, and our dismay at the lack of action and urgency was still fresh in our minds. The callous disregard for our well-being was never more apparent than what formed in every wrinkle on the CEO's face. When Beatrice spoke at last, her voice—usually so full of lively confidence that it could calm a distressed patient in seconds—was tinged with exasperation.

"It was like talking to a brick wall," she said, finally stopping her pacing and turning to face me. "John Pearson simply doesn't see why any of this matters, why we matter. It's disheartening."

Beatrice had been at the forefront of these negotiations with the CEO, and her passion for the cause was evident in every word she spoke. Yet, all her efforts were met with deflections, non-committal nods, and a general unwillingness to lean into the issues.

"Bea, you're doing everything right," I began, choosing my words carefully. "The way you speak up, the arguments you present, your advocacy... it's all impressive. You're taking on a role many have shied away from because of what it takes to do it right. These things take time, and people at the top can resist change, like we saw."

She sighed heavily, dropping into a chair next to me.

"I know. Our friends and colleagues will suffer every day we are delayed: long shifts, inadequate rest, constant pressure. How long before someone else gets hurt? We can't just be idle and hope things get better. Clearly, this country's healthcare system doesn't prioritize what's best for patients and professionals, so I will not be foolish enough to expect anything different here in Frieden Bay."

Her voice cracked slightly, and her eyes, usually so bright, looked tired.

"You've started something consequential here," I said firmly. "You've rallied the residents and brought issues to light that were ignored for too long. And, yes, I agree that this should be straightforward. But without you, there would be no conversation or progress at all. You're not just a leader; you're an inspiration, Bea."

Her eyes met mine, and I could see the flicker of resolve reigniting.

"You think so?"

"I know so," I assured her. "You have a lot of fans, Dr. Portinari. You have a lot of people who look up to you and want to follow your example."

A small smile tugged at the corners of her lips.

"That's so sweet for you to say."

"You won't stop here," I continued. "We'll draft another proposal, gather more signatures, and show more evidence. We'll make it impossible for them to ignore us."

Beatrice leaned back, the weight of the world lifting off her shoulders a bit.

"I'm fortunate to have you. Thank you for believing in the union and me."

"Always," I replied. "You lead. I'll have your back as your co-resident. You speak, I'll echo. Together, we'll make them listen."

As I watched her sit up straighter, her demeanor slowly shifting from defeat to tenacity, I knew that no matter how tough the CEO was, he had not reckoned with the kind of force that was Beatrice. She was a leader through and through, and I was proud to stand by her side. As we chatted and had cups of fresh, black coffee, the scent of the coffee hit my nose and gave me with a warm feeling, which evoked memories of late winter nights in my college's library when I would drink copious amounts of coffee to fight off my weariness and focus on my term papers.

Suddenly, I was transported back to sitting with Dr. Altamura and my co-residents on *The Albatross*, bearing our souls and pledging to be there for one another. The promise Dr. Altamura had us make still resounded in my mind: "Promise me that you will always look out for one another as brothers and sisters. The bond you will develop with one another in your training will be unrivaled, and you must cherish it." With Dr. Altamura gone, I felt more committed to this promise than ever.

We knew we had the power of numbers on our side. I helped Beatrice organize rallies with the residents and other Alta Vista employees, reach out to different organizations to build partnerships, and garner support from our specialty societies. As the days turned into weeks, the pressure on the CEO and senior leadership continued to mount. The union's message spread like wildfire, and public opinion was entirely on our side. Slowly but surely, the CEO began to realize that he could no longer ignore the voices of his employees.

After weeks of negotiations and countless hours of debate, the hospital finally agreed to recognize the medical trainee union and enter into collective bargaining with them. Improved working conditions and better patient care were finally within reach, thanks to the tireless efforts of Beatrice and the union members. As the news spread throughout the hospital, there was a sense of triumph and satisfaction among the union members. We had fought long and hard for our rights, and our perseverance had paid off. The union brought positive change within the hospital, setting a powerful example for healthcare professionals. Our next goal was to secure protections for residents working in the hospital and bring justice for Leslie, ensuring nobody else would fall victim to a dysfunctional system.

Despite our victories as a union, the weight of Dr. Altamura's death continued to bear down on me. I had always prided myself on resilience, on the ability to handle whatever came my way. This time, it was different; this cut was deeper and harder to heal. I remembered my previous encounters with therapists during the chaotic days of college and understood that it was time to seek help again. Using my recently improved employee benefits, I reached out. I connected with Dr. Melanie Price, a reputed psychiatrist at Alta Vista Hospital specializing in behavioral medicine for healthcare professionals and their families.

Dr. Price's office starkly contrasted the rest of the hospital; it was warm and inviting, filled with pastel colors and gentle lighting. Sitting across from her, nestled in an armchair that seemed to swallow my stress temporarily, I felt an odd mix of relief and apprehension.

"Tell me what brings you here," Dr. Price began, her voice calm and grounding, her eyes understanding yet professionally detached.

I related the recent events and my feelings toward them. Dr. Price listened intently, occasionally taking notes. I talked about the disturbing death of Dr. Altamura before covering more recent events. The sudden demise of a titan of family medicine left me feeling remarkably hollow and incomplete. My mentor had been wrested from my hands, and it felt like the universe had just kicked me to the curb.

"I think not being able to attend his funeral and get closure has complicated my grieving," I disclosed, staring down at my open hands. "The last time I saw him, he was doing well. And then, he was gone in the blink of an eye."

"That must have been very difficult for you to go through, especially with the expectations that he was getting better," Dr. Price scrunched her brow. "What have you been doing to navigate these complicated emotions?"

We explored coping mechanisms, from maintaining open conversations with colleagues who felt similarly and forming a support group to journaling my thoughts and feelings. Dr. Price emphasized the importance of building resilience: not by hardening myself against emotional pain but by allowing myself to experience and process these emotions in a healthy and psychologically safe environment.

That evening, I shaved my face before heading off to bed. I played some soft rock music to fill the silence of my apartment and gently bobbed my head to the familiar tunes. As I rinsed the shaving cream and loose hairs off, I looked up toward the mirror. Perhaps it was just blurry vision from the water, but something in the reflection made my heart skip a beat. I was looking at myself, but there seemed to be a shadow over my face. It lasted for only a split second. I hastily dried off my face and shut the bathroom door behind me on my way out. By the time I slipped into bed and closed my eyes, I had forgotten all about the shadow.

CHAPTER ELEVEN

Much-Needed Reminder

> *The fool proclaims itself an ascendant and carries out its ritual of self-deceit, confidently trying to produce wings from its body. When no wings emerge, the fool proceeds to repeat the ritual over and over again, expecting different outcomes each time it does.*

In March of my second year, my rural work assignment took me to a community at the base of a colossal mountain range hundreds of miles away, where skiing and snowboarding were common pastimes and vital components of the local economy. In my barely passable front-wheel drive vehicle, I made my way carefully through winding roads covered in snow and potholes, determined to reach the community and settle into a kind woman's guesthouse for the month. As I drove, the surrounding landscape transformed before my eyes. The sprawling fields and small houses gradually gave way to towering blue spruce trees that stood proudly, their branches draped with a thick veil of snow. The air grew colder and drier, and I felt tranquility as I took in the stunning wintry scenery.

Finally, after what felt like a lifetime, I arrived at the community of Oktusha. It was a quaint little town at the foot of the majestic mountain range. Charming cottages with roofs weighed down by the heavy snow lined the streets. Smoke billowed from chimneys, creating a cozy ambiance that immediately made me feel at home. I parked my car in the gravel-laden driveway of the guesthouse I would stay in for the month. It was a modest building with heating and an unparalleled view of the mountains. Across from it was the main house where Mrs. Abigail Davis lived. As I stepped up on the front porch and rang the doorbell, I was greeted by warmth and comfort that embraced me like an old friend. After inviting me in for a cup of coffee and a slice of quiche, Mrs. Davis handed me the key to the guesthouse and wished me luck on my rural assignment.

The guesthouse was small but incredibly cozy, with a full kitchen, decorated tile floors, and a queen-size platform bed with a perfectly firm mattress. As I acclimated to the altitude and the new living space, I experienced almost indescribable tranquility in knowing I had the perfect place to escape after a long day of work up in the ski valley. My specific assignment involved working in an urgent care clinic that functioned as an emergency department where most cases were acute musculoskeletal injuries. Previous residents had described the rotation as indispensable for anybody who wanted to hone their clinical skills in diagnosing and managing acute orthopedic issues, such as fractures and dislocations.

The following day, I woke up to a winter wonderland. A fresh layer of soft, powdery snow blanketed the mostly unpaved streets, and the mountain peaks glistened under the morning sun. I made my way to the clinic with a cup of steaming hot coffee. Located adjacent to the main ski lifts, it was a spacious clinic: it contained a central atrium with a high ceiling and skylights that splintered off into individual triage and exam bays, with separate rooms for trauma and resuscitation. When I arrived, the clinic staff welcomed me with open arms: curious about my training goals and eager to share their stories about Oktusha, the mountains, and shredding down the slopes on skis. Within about five minutes of arriving, Dr. Andrea Larrabee entered through the back doors, dressed in her ski goggles, beanie, and heavy jacket.

"Welcome to La Vida en la Nieve Urgent Care Clinic!" Dr. Larrabee warmly announced to me from across the atrium. "You must be the new resident with whom I have been emailing for several weeks."

"That's right," I responded animatedly. "I'm looking forward to this rural rotation."

Taking advantage of the morning lull, Dr. Larrabee sat down with me in her small office and explained her clinic role and the rotation expectations. She stated that I needed to focus on quick thinking and acute clinical skills to manage the injuries and other acute issues that came through the door each day. She stressed that she anticipated a high volume of patients during my rotation because many tourists and "fair-weather snowhounds" would be skiing and snowboarding during spring break. Dr. Larrabee walked me through the various clinical areas, pointing out essential equipment like the X-ray machine, crash cart, splinting and casting materials, and suturing supplies. We moseyed over to the break room, where she offered me some pistachios before the day got busy.

By the early afternoon, the clinic was bursting at the seams with patients with various complaints and mechanisms of injury. First, there was an avid snowboarder with a non-displaced distal radial fracture. Then, there was a skier who had taken a nasty fall on the moguls and sustained an acute anterior shoulder dislocation. I had to move quickly from patient to patient, lining people up for X-rays and preparing for dislocation reductions. Every case sharpened my skills throughout that first day and deepened my understanding of musculoskeletal medicine in such a remote, high-impact environment.

One patient, a young woman with a shy smile, caught me off-guard. She had twisted her knee when she came down hard from a large slope toward the top of the main mountain. It was not severe, but after examining her knee carefully, I found she had sprained her anterior cruciate and medial collateral ligaments. As I explained the need for a hinged knee brace, non-steroidal anti-inflammatory medications, and contrast baths, our conversation drifted to the extraordinary beauty of the mountains.

"Even though I often get hurt, I still come every season," she said, her eyes brightening with every word. "You get to see things nobody else can see from the peaks of these mountains. There is nothing like slicing through fresh powder and doing one of the most exhilarating activities in the world. Risky or not, it makes you feel alive."

Even though I was not a skier or snowboarder, I could still understand what people were getting from being up on the mountain: finding the *joie de vivre* in the unadulterated wilderness. The conversation I had with that young woman lingered in my mind as I continued my day—splinting fractures, bracing sprains, and reducing dislocated bones. Each patient added a brick to the foundation of my growing expertise in this area of medicine.

Evenings in the guesthouse were blissful. As twilight fell over the mountains, I would sit in the backroom near one of the windows and watch a kaleidoscope of color dance along the ridges of the mountains, rising like imperial figures on the horizon. Once night had fallen, I would entertain myself with a good movie on my laptop until I fell asleep. The crisp mountain air, the quiet, and the satisfaction of helping those in need intertwined, weaving together contentment and belonging. Day after day, I felt myself growing as a clinician and discovered some new elements I loved about working in healthcare.

On the Friday of my first week, I was chatting with Chase Manning, a perky and affable physician assistant who had grown up in Seattle. His young son and wife came by to visit while getting everything together for a fun day of skiing. As we exchanged stories and discussed complex health policy issues affecting patients and clinicians across the country, the harsh white noise of the clinic radio interrupted us.

"Ski patrol to La Nieve, come in," a high-pitched voice called across the radio.

Chase hurried over to the radio to receive the report. Ski patrol stated that they had found a fourteen-year-old girl down near some trees in the valley. The urgency in the patroller's voice sent a chill down my spine as I prepared myself for the worst. Moments later, we received the devastating news that she was apneic and pulseless, suspected to have sustained a direct tree strike. Shortly after, we learned that someone initiated CPR and placed an automated external defibrillator in the field. Dread paralyzed me when the ski patrol told us the automated defibrillator did not advise a shock. This strongly suggested that she was either in asystole or possibly pulseless electrical activity, neither of which were survivable cardiac arrhythmias. Fear coursed through my veins like icy tendrils as I realized the gravity of the situation.

After taking the full report from the ski patrol, Chase was urgently called to the scene, accompanied by a nurse and an emergency physician who were already there. The severity of the girl's condition felt like an elephant standing on our chests as we braced ourselves for the worst possible outcome at the clinic. The thought of losing someone so young and full of life was a bitter and jagged pill to swallow, and I shuddered at the idea of having to perform resuscitative interventions to bring someone like that back to life.

Silence fell over the clinic for about ten minutes. As we waited with bated breath, I realized I was the only provider left at the clinic, meaning I would need to lead any necessary codes if she remained unresponsive. I was in the company of a paramedic and two ski patrollers. Time seemed to stretch infinitely as we anxiously awaited any news about the girl. Eventually, we received word that a ski patroller was heading back to the clinic. With no further information, we jumped into action when we saw the sled carrying the girl arrive.

Working swiftly, we transported her inside and rushed her to the trauma room. The sight we beheld was enough to freeze the blood in our veins. I removed the blanket covering her and conducted a brief assessment, taking the lead in what I believed to be the continuation of the code started in the field. She was severely hypothermic. Her breathing ceased, her pulse was nonexistent, and blood obstructed her throat and congealed around her mouth. The injuries she sustained were beyond gruesome, immediately leaving an image of her cadaveric face burned into my brain.

I wasted no time in attempting to clear her airway, suctioning her mouth and throat with minimal success before painstakingly readjusting her jaw to insert a laryngeal mask airway safely. While the paramedic continued chest compressions, I attempted to ventilate through the advanced airway. Despite addressing her airway, the copious amounts of blood hindered my efforts, with gushes of frank blood flashing up into her nostrils with each artificial breath. With desperation mounting, I called for the insertion of an intravenous or intraosseous line to administer epinephrine, hoping for a glimmer of response. Meanwhile, one of the ski patrollers attached leads to monitor her cardiac activity. Unfortunately, the monitor confirmed my suspicion: she was in asystole. The resuscitation attempt went on for what felt like an eternity.

After nine minutes, the emergency physician who responded to the scene arrived. Only then did we discover that resuscitation had already been terminated in the field without our knowledge. The physician halted our efforts, revealing that several interventions had been performed during the traumatic arrest, of which we were unaware. In the following debriefing, it came to light that communication had failed, resulting in the clinic lacking necessary updates for approximately fifteen minutes. It was likely that this young girl had died instantaneously upon impact, her fate sealed by a severe cardiac contusion, traumatic brain injury, or a combination of injuries.

Though we did what was necessary in the heat of the moment, our actions were ultimately futile in the face of the harsh reality that she was already dead before she reached us. The team acknowledged our efforts, recognizing that we had done all we could in the clinic. However, I found myself wrestling with indescribable anger and sorrow, deeply affected by what I witnessed and the desperate actions I had to take for a young life that was already tragically extinguished. Night after night, nightmares plagued my sleep, and even in waking moments, flashes of her face haunted me, constantly reminding me of the fragility of life.

I STOOD ON THE SANDS OF A DISTANT ISLAND IN THE Pacific Ocean, basking in the gorgeous and brilliant sunlight. It was a small paradise, barely a blip on most maps, with dense forests fringing its shores and only a small population. Life was easy, days slipping by with the timeless rhythm of the tides. The young girl was there, her laughter mingling with the lap of small waves caressing the beach. She frolicked by the water's edge, her hands shaping the wet sand into elaborate castles adorned with shells and driftwood. Enjoying the pure, unguarded moments of her childhood, she remained blissfully unaware of the changing sky.

Without warning, vicious storm clouds stained red and black gathered on the horizon, transforming day into night. My gaze was fixed in horror as a giant wave—an embodiment of Poseidon's wrath—reared about a mile away. The tsunami churned with unstoppable fury and approached with relentless speed. With her focus attuned to her miniature sand empire, the young girl did not notice the danger brewing. The deafening roar of the assembling thunder drowned out my frantic calls to her.

"Run away!" I cried, my voice lost in the violent orchestration of impending doom.

Panicking, the other villagers and I surged forward, our legs pumping in desperation across the sand, trying to bridge the gap between the girl and us. However, nature's cruel spectacle did not afford us the luxury of a miracle. The monstrous wave swallowed her whole in a grave of frothy water, and then, with the voracity of a beast unleashed, it turned its rage upon us. The water hit like a freight train, dismantling everything in its path—homes, trees, memories. I remember tumbling in the aquatic turmoil, saltwater filling my lungs, my body battered by debris. I saw Dr. Altamura's lifeless body sinking to the bottom of the ocean before everything slipped into darkness.

The days following her death were haunting. I was not interested in discussing what had transpired, lest I re-experience that horrific moment. The next day, I arrived at work a little late with the oppressive weight of the traumatic event on my mind. As I walked through the clinic doors, I could feel the eyes of my relatively new colleagues on me. Some offered sympathetic nods, while others simply averted their gaze. Dr. Larrabee was waiting for me at my desk. Her normally composed and confident demeanor was replaced with one of worry.

"How're you doing?" she asked gently, her voice filled with concern.

I sighed and looked down at my feet, unprepared to confront the emotions that threatened to overwhelm me.

"I'm okay," I responded dismissively, hoping to brush off the conversation I knew we needed to have.

Dr. Larrabee was not easily deterred. She knew what trauma could do to people and understood the stormy interior behind a calm exterior following a traumatic experience. With a pertinacious expression on her face, she took a seat beside me and placed a comforting hand on my shoulder.

"I know 'okay' can mean many things," she said softly. "But I also know that losing someone so young is never easy. This is especially true when the circumstances are traumatic."

Her words hit me harder than I expected. The floodgates of emotions that I had attempted to keep locked inside came rushing forth, and tears filled my eyes. The pain that I had been trying to hide suddenly became too much to handle.

Dr. Larrabee pulled me into a calming embrace, letting me relinquish some of the burdens I had been carrying. Her silent understanding and unwavering support provided the solace I desperately needed. We sat there in silence, breathing in the mutually understood pain and finding strength in each other's presence.

"After everything you've been through, it's important to allow yourself to grieve," Dr. Larrabee spoke softly and empathetically. "This isn't something you have to face alone. We're here for you every step of the way."

Her words felt like a lifeline, pulling me out of despair. I nodded, grateful for the support she offered. In the days that followed, Dr. Larrabee became my rock. She guided me through the challenging process of grieving and healing. Our conversations provided an outlet for my jumbled thoughts and emotions, helping me make sense of the tragedy that had unfolded. Dr. Larrabee encouraged me to seek professional help, reminding me that true healing required more than just leaning on someone like her. I assured her I already had access to therapy resources, which would be instrumental in my long-term recovery.

As time passed, the intensity of the pain began to wane, replaced by memories of happier times. Dr. Larrabee and I continued to work together in the clinic, our bond growing stronger with each passing day. I realized that the days following the young girl's death were not just haunting but also transformative. The grief I experienced had reshaped my perspective and priorities—much like when I lost Dr. Altamura. It deepened my empathy and understanding for others who faced loss and trauma. Through my journey, I discovered the power of support, compassion, and connection.

Looking back, that difficult conversation with Dr. Larrabee was a turning point. It was the moment I allowed myself to open up and accept help, to acknowledge that healing was a process that required vulnerability. In her gentle guidance, I found the strength to rebuild and find hope. As I returned to work each day, bearing the weight of the traumatic event on my mind, I knew I was not alone. Dr. Larrabee was always there, ready to listen, guide, and remind me that healing was possible, even if I sometimes had my doubts about that.

Several days after the fatal tree strike that claimed the young girl's life, I scheduled a virtual appointment with Dr. Price for therapy. Ahead of the session, I sent Dr. Price a secure message to give an overview of that fateful Friday. Despite my continuing conversations with Dr. Larrabee and the others at the ski valley clinic, I was still struggling with the effects of trauma from having led the code on that child. This incident felt even more difficult after losing Dr. Altamura not so long ago.

The day of my appointment was bleak, with heavy snow falling from the sky. The room was quiet except for the occasional droning of the furnace from across the guesthouse. My laptop screen flickered as I logged into the virtual meeting platform. At precisely 10:00 am, Dr. Price's face appeared on the screen; her smile was gentle, and her eyes were keen and observing.

"It's been tough, Dr. Price," I admitted, my voice cracking. "I keep reliving the scene—the sounds, the cold, that helpless feeling."

"Flashbacks are common after traumatic experiences, especially for medical professionals in intense situations," Dr. Price commented earnestly. "Tell me: what emotions come up when you think about the incident?"

I hesitated, searching for the right words. I inhaled deeply, exhaustion and grief clamping down on my chest and throat.

"Guilt, primarily. And anger. I am angry at myself for not being able to save her. I am angry at those who did not communicate with us at the clinic. I am angry at the universe for taking away Dr. Altamura and this young girl."

"It's understandable," Dr. Price responded, leaning toward her webcam. "You're dealing not only with the fresh trauma but also unresolved grief from losing a mentor. It's a lot for anyone, particularly someone in your line of work. You're expected to save lives, but some factors are beyond your control."

As we delved deeper into the session, Dr. Price guided me through a cognitive restructuring exercise. This exercise addressed my self-blame and helped me differentiate between my responsibilities and the unpredictable forces of nature and accidents.

"The guilt you feel is a testament to your empathy and dedication," Dr. Price explained. "However, it's important to remember that you did everything within your power. I want you to work on forgiving yourself and understanding that sometimes, despite all our efforts, the outcome is not what we hope for."

The session progressed with discussions about coping mechanisms, such as mindfulness and scheduled downtime, to help manage my stress levels. Dr. Price also suggested journaling my thoughts and the events as a form of processing the trauma.

"I'm here when you need to talk, but I also encourage you to lean on your peers who might be experiencing similar feelings," Dr. Price advised. "Sometimes, sharing with those who understand the context can also be helpful."

"I've been doing that with Dr. Larrabee and the others who went through this," I shared with her, feeling more confident now.

After logging off, I sat back on the bed, feeling slightly lighter. The conversation with Dr. Price had opened a small window of relief in the oppressive room of my mind. I scribbled down the appointment I had scheduled for our next session, finding peace in the continuity.

That evening, I decided to visit the ski valley clinic. Dr. Larrabee was there, and after seeing her, I felt an urge to relate the insights from my session with Dr. Price.

"You know," I began as we had tea in the break room, "I spoke with my psychiatrist today about the incident. She helped me see some things in a different light."

Dr. Larrabee listened—her eyes soft, understanding.

"I'm glad to hear that. It's important to take care of your mental health. We're here together in this."

Dr. Larrabee's words were a much-needed reminder of what I valued so much about healthcare: connection with others.

CHAPTER
TWELVE

BITTERSWEET

> *What the fool will never understand in its waking stupor is that nature forbids any change without due resistance; nature demands stability in a structure that is productive and sustainable.*

One morning in May, just before dawn, I sluggishly lifted myself out of bed, wrapped a large blanket around myself, and hobbled over to my range to boil water for my coffee. I donned my headphones to play nostalgic music from the mid-1990s as I completed a few outstanding office visit notes. I lazily nibbled on two slices of toast slathered in avocado and poppy seeds. Despite the hassle of completing my documentation after a day in the clinic, this was an appropriate tradeoff for being more present with my patients during their visits. Slowly but surely, I was becoming concise in my notes, communicating what was essential for billing and consistent healthcare from one provider to the next.

Today was my turn to bring in candies and other delectable treats for the staff at our clinic, so I collected two hefty grocery bags filled with assorted goodies before getting in my car. After arriving in the clinic workroom, I noticed Dr. Calisto and his nearly six and a half feet of height, almost dwarfing the door frame of the program office. In the corner of the workroom, Vincent and Soraya huddled around a computer, loudly cackling at a new video Soraya found online. Lisa, the nurse in our clinic, was carrying several boxes of new intrauterine contraceptive devices across the room to a nearby medical supply storage closet. I saw a card from one of our medical assistants on my keyboard, which contained a heartwarming thank-you message for all of the moral support as she started her new job in a different city.

The beauty of primary care was never more apparent in my work than today: my whole morning consisted of visits with patients I had been seeing since I first moved to Frieden Bay. Nothing was quite as satisfying as seeing long-term care plans come to fruition and developing strong relationships with them. At this point, I could have honest and respectful conversations with my patients, discussing things that would have otherwise been hard to bring up. Beyond confidently talking with them, I was starting to feel like their doctor instead of someone who was just peripherally involved in their care, parroting the recommendations of the preceptor. While I appreciated the wisdom and guidance of our attending physicians, this growing sense of accountability and autonomy over my patients' care was crucial for my growth as a professional and left me feeling much more self-actualized.

During lunch, Beatrice, Vincent, Soraya, and I joked with one another and made predictions about who would be doing what in just over a year. From outside the workroom, I could still hear Dr. Calisto having an indiscernible conversation with someone whose voice I could not recognize. It was odd because Dr. Calisto generally had meetings and discussions with higher-ups at the hospital in his office on the other side of the clinic space. Without any clear-cut reason to be concerned, I shrugged it off and continued bantering with my co-residents. After returning to my desk to gather some supplies for a skin biopsy, I detected a prominent figure approaching from my peripheral vision. With no one else in the room, I turned quickly to see Dr. Calisto standing there, his ordinary cheeriness wiped from his face.

"I need to tell you something," he said flatly. "I was..."

Although he clearly articulated the last word, every sympathetic nerve in my body fired at precisely the same time, sending my heart into overdrive, filling my ears with its rapid beating, and slowing my verbal comprehension to a snail's pace. Time seemed to slow around us like we were standing in an extradimensional bubble. Recognizing my own failing senses and wanting to compensate for them, I gleaned what information I could by using my vision instead: the glassy eyes, the redness of the periorbital skin, the clear discharge from the nose, the furrowed brow.

Oh, please, no, I thought, panic-stricken. *There's no way.*

"They said this was a no-cause termination, which is mostly corporate speak for 'We are not going to tell you why we came to this decision.'"

Fired. That was the word: fired.

"I'll talk with your Chief about organizing a meeting with the residents after everyone finishes their work. It would be unofficial because senior leadership does not want me to speak too openly with the residents or program staff."

I nodded at Dr. Calisto, unable to utter a single syllable through the vise gripping my throat. I was flabbergasted, overwhelmed by the wave of dread for our future as a program that engulfed my mind. I waved goodbye to Dr. Calisto as he left, shoulders slumped forward in an unceremonious defeat.

That evening, Brett, the current Chief Resident of our program, organized a virtual meeting to update us on what was known about Dr. Calisto's termination and the next steps. Between the outraged statements from the junior and senior residents, we learned that two leadership team members from Alta Vista offered to meet with us to answer questions and address concerns about Dr. Calisto's sudden termination. He offered his support to anyone in our group who needed it. In many ways, it felt like we were delivering an elegy for someone who had died.

All residents were excused from their clinical duties on Wednesday morning to attend the meeting with senior leadership, ostensibly ready to set the record straight on the bombshell that rocked the residency just a few days prior. Our conference room—where ebullience usually prevailed—felt eerily more akin to a morgue as residents from all three years shuffled into the room. They noiselessly took their seats, engaging minimally with those around them. I sat down opposite where the two hospital leaders placed themselves at the head of the table. I wanted to listen to their responses from a good, safe distance.

"Good morning, everyone." A woman dressed in a plaid pantsuit stood up and addressed us. "I am Norma Fredrickson with the Alta Vista Hospital Senior Leadership Team. While many of you may not know me, I am in charge of physician employment at this facility. I am joined today by Dr. Orlando Klein, our Chief Clinical Officer."

As they waved out at the group, I could see scowls forming on the faces of several of our senior residents, including Brett's. Perhaps calling these two people unpopular would have been an understatement. The room became so tense in a trice that one could slice it with a knife.

"We are here to talk with you about the recent termination of Dr. Alexander Calisto," Norma continued in a stilted and monotone manner. "We realize that this came as a shock to most—if not all—of you. Dr. Calisto had been working with Alta Vista Hospital for over fifteen years, over ten of which were spent as Program Director."

"This was a decision we did not make lightly," Dr. Klein finally said. "Dr. Calisto is an asset to our community and will be deeply missed. With that, do you all—"

"Why did this happen?" Brett interjected, barely able to restrain himself. "What was wrong with what Dr. Calisto was doing?"

Norma smirked, seemingly getting smug satisfaction from the emotions in the room.

"We cannot fully disclose the termination details; that would breach Dr. Calisto's privacy. Dr. Klein and I had numerous conversations with Dr. Calisto about what we were looking for with the program. Ultimately, we just needed a change of direction in leadership."

What does that even mean? I thought, squinting my eyes at the speakers in front of us.

"Come on, now," Vincent retorted incredulously. "I thought you said you were here to answer questions. You all really can't give more information than that?"

"Did I not answer your colleague's question?" Norma condescended, narrowing her eyes at Vincent. "Look, Dr. Klein and I cannot reveal all the details to you. That would violate our ethical and contractual duties to Alta Vista."

Over the next forty minutes, Norma and Dr. Klein deflected and avoided every question, choosing instead to shovel in statements of their "commitment" to the residency program and how "important" the residents are to the local community. Despite the trenchant criticisms of the decision raised by the residents, the senior leaders before us made one thing abundantly clear: they were not going to budge.

"I didn't realize it was even possible to say so little with so many words," Vincent shook his head, glaring at the ground. "And to gaslight every person so badly for so long. Bastards."

Stunned and appalled by my lack of control at the moment, all I could muster was a simple nod to signify my solidarity with him.

Dr. Coffman had sent out an intentionally vague email the evening before, which quickly became the main topic of discussion in the physician's lounge at the hospital. Speculations ran rampant among the residents, fueled by curiosity, acrimony, and caffeine.

By the time we had all crowded into the modest lounge, the meeting space was stifling. Dr. Coffman wasted no time, making the major announcements right off the bat. Many residents felt vulnerable and perturbed without Dr. Calisto, who had been a stalwart mentor and a shield against the more cumbersome administrative policies.

"As you all know, Dr. Calisto's departure leaves us with a vacant core faculty position," Dr. Coffman stated, reading the room as he spoke. "We're actively looking for someone to fill his position, acknowledging how hard it will be to find someone with his unique combination of qualities as an educator and leader."

Murmurs erupted across the room before Dr. Coffman gestured for silence.

"And I must address the rumor that's been circulating: we have offered Dr. Calisto's role to an internal candidate. After careful consideration, Dr. Mose has accepted the position of Program Director."

Dr. Coffman paused after the first news round, apparently measuring the reaction. I felt a brew of emotions inside myself—the instability of the situation gave me some reservations about any changes. This announcement was truly bittersweet.

With her balanced approach to problem-solving and progressive thinking, Dr. Mose's appointment as the new Program Director was a consolation. She had been instrumental in advocating for residents' rights and improving work-life balance within our rigorous program. However, Dr. Calisto had been a favorite among the residents. He often stayed late after giving lectures and seeing patients to chat with residents about their personal problems. When budget cuts threatened to restrict official programming last year, Dr. Calisto fought to reverse the administrators' decisions. His dedication to education and resident welfare was unparalleled.

After the announcement, Dr. Coffman opened the floor for residents to ask questions. Vincent raised his hand, the conflict in his mind propelling him forward.

"With Dr. Calisto now gone and Dr. Mose stepping up, how do you all intend to ensure that the leadership transition does not disrupt residents' educational experiences?"

It was the question on many lips based on the chorus of murmurs around him.

Dr. Mose answered this question—her voice filled with an understanding that only someone who had been through the grind as she had could exhibit.

"I appreciate your concern, Vincent," she said. "I was a resident once. I understand the pressures and the stakes. We are prioritizing a seamless transition. Moreover, I intend to uphold and, whenever possible, build on Dr. Calisto's initiatives toward better clinical rotations, more resident leadership opportunities, and resident wellness."

Ultimately, her assurances were met with tentative hope. The meeting adjourned with Dr. Coffman's promise of open doors for any further questions or concerns. As the residents filed out of the cramped room, I lingered, my thoughts still racing. I remembered Dr. Calisto's most influential words about always finding ways to innovate and improve, no matter how harrowing the journey. With Dr. Mose at the helm, adapting to the changes seemed less daunting, but some doubts and uncertainty about the future remained. The egregious disregard for graduate medical education from individuals representing corporatized healthcare and its profit-driven motives had the residents keyed up and afraid. Change would always be a double-edged sword, but perhaps it could be wielded wisely and righteously with Dr. Mose's guidance.

A WEEK HAD PASSED SINCE THE DEMORALIZING MEETING with hospital leadership about Dr. Calisto's termination. While I had all the confidence in the world about Dr. Mose in her new role as Program Director, something was disconcerting about losing a man who had given so much to us as residents. The emotional toll was heavier than mere words could convey. Dr. Calisto was not just a mentor but a beacon of kindness in the relentless storm of residency. His office was a sanctuary where residents found courage and wisdom. Now, that office lay empty in the throes of an inexplicably forced transition.

The decision to terminate him, based on alleged policy violations that few could substantiate, struck a nerve with everyone. Understandably, his departure created a void that seemed to darken the hallways of the hospital and clinic. After he left, I realized the scale of the situation's impact on me. I could no longer brush aside the curt nods in the hallway and sorrow-laden sighs. Moreover, the death of Dr. Altamura, another pillar of moral and educational support, had begun to wear down my resilience.

It was not just the loss of Dr. Calisto but the crumbling of an ideal that troubled me. His firing represented a loss of what I believed medicine should be—an art and science guided by compassion and ethics rather than a bureaucracy stiffened by policies and market pressures.

"It sounds like you're grappling with what's often called 'moral injury,'" Dr. Price observed when I finished updating her. "It's when we feel betrayed by authorities or systems that are supposed to uphold certain ethical standards."

I nodded. That was precisely it: betrayal. I felt betrayed by the system and its sycophantic suits.

"Moral injury can be tough because it shakes the foundation of our moral and ethical beliefs. Healing begins with acknowledging this pain and understanding that feeling let down is okay," she continued, offering validation.

The moral injury was real: a deep-seated malaise that went beyond the ordinary stresses of a demanding career. The struggle to adapt to the new dynamics in the hospital after Dr. Calisto's departure persisted. However, each day, I found a renewed sense of purpose. It was not just about filling the void he left behind; it was about redefining it, creating a space where the next generation of healthcare professionals could learn to navigate their moral landscapes without losing sight of why they chose to wear the white coat in the first place.

Chapter Thirteen

The World I Know

> *If one could elicit change without encountering opposition, then life would feel hollow and devoid of purpose. The universe cannot harbor disorderly disorder—it would implode under the unfathomable weight of unchecked entropy.*

The hot water splashed over my chest as I stepped into the shower, a cascading relief after a long, tiring day. It was the end of another rotation, and I had just arrived back after my last day of work. I continued to practice my coping strategies on the long drive back, having made a lot of progress in controlling my posttraumatic symptoms. I would focus on belly breathing when my heart would start racing randomly. I would breathe into a small sachet of lavender to ground myself when

I began to lose control of my thoughts. I would never forget what happened on the mountain, but eventually, I could live life with that experience being a well-compartmentalized part of my memory. I could be damaged but not broken, which gave me the courage to confront my mind's troubling dissonance.

I savored every moment of standing in the shower, long enough for the steam to fog up the entire bathroom. Reluctantly, I turned off the heavenly water and reached for my towel. The faint lingering of citrus, teak, and sandalwood fragrance from my shampoo and body wash filled the air, wrapping me in a cocoon of easement. As I dried off, I noticed the condensation had formed a thick layer on the mirror, blurring my reflection and entrancing me with its cloudy appearance. Like a rock sailing through a glass house, the harsh sound of my phone ringing broke my trance.

"Are you on your way?" Vincent shouted over the phone, the blaring pop music and loud conversations nearly drowning out his voice.

"Yeah, I just got back an hour ago," I responded, brushing my hair. "I'm just getting ready. I'll be there soon. Remind me: you all are at the beach, right?"

"That is correct," he replied slowly, distracted by something around him. "Park near the piers, and I'll meet you there."

"Got it. I'll let you go so I can hurry and finish here."

Hanging up, I hastily wrapped the towel around me and entered my bedroom to get dressed. Standing in front of my closet, I suddenly realized that my wardrobe was diametrically split between T-shirts and dress shirts without much in between for a party. I dug through the back of my closet until I found a floral-print button-up shirt and suitable denim jeans. I threw on my clothes and sprayed on a few spritzes of cologne. Pulling out the hard lemonades I got for tonight from the refrigerator, I grabbed my keys, phone, and wallet and then headed out the door.

Since I had been so busy with this month's rotation, I had almost forgotten how relaxing it was to drive across the town at night and down to the beach. I rested my head on my left fist as I watched the yellow orbs of light from the lampposts pass by me into the calm blackness of the night. As I pulled into a parking spot near the piers, I glimpsed from afar the large pergola under which a group of my co-residents were gathered together, surrounded by strings of fairy lights that cast a soft, dreamlike glow. The salty breeze from the sea mingled with the laughter and music, creating an environment that felt otherworldly and inviting.

"Over here!" Vincent called out, waving and jogging over to my location. "It's good to see you again. It feels like a year since I last saw you."

"How're you holding up, brother?" I checked in with him, giving Vincent a tight hug.

"I'm managing," he replied, motioning at the pergola to get us moving in that direction. "My girlfriend of four weeks and I broke up yesterday. It wasn't working out, but I was still sad to see the relationship fall apart."

"I'm sorry about that, Vin," I said gently. "You'll find someone else. That's more of a reason for us to have fun tonight."

When we arrived at the pergola, I was welcomed by everyone hanging out, drinking, and munching on finger foods. I checked in with the other residents before moseying over to join Soraya and Beatrice, who were nestled into cushioned rattan armchairs. I hugged each of them before claiming my armchair and briefly updating them on my outpatient pediatrics rotation. Reaching from behind me, Vincent handed me a mixed drink: a tangy mélange of lemon and mint with a punch of vodka.

"This is delicious," I said, turning to Vincent as he threw himself on the last available rattan armchair. "What is this?"

"Vin-ka's Juice," he replied with a straight face, sipping the same concoction from an identical glass. "Well, I just got a little creative with what I had at home. I'm glad you like it."

Vincent made an impromptu toast to the three of us before quickly returning to his cozy seat.

"It's really nice to catch up with you all," Vincent remarked, stretching his arms high above his head. "Sometimes, it gets so lonely in the freaking hospital, even in the company of all of the other staff. How have you all been?"

"About as well as we can be right now," Soraya chimed in, looking intently at her plate of celery, carrots, and fried chicken wings. "Our daughter is doing well in school despite the recent statewide cuts to the education budget. Her teachers have been so good; they have been so resourceful in keeping learning fun for the kids, despite all of the barriers."

"That's been such an embarrassment for our state," Beatrice sighed and shook her head, taking a large sip from one of the hard lemonades I brought. "Thank you for bringing these, by the way! They're my favorite."

Now fully settled in at the party, we chatted about the others' recent rotations. Soraya spent the month working with an endocrinologist in private practice, who gave her valuable insights into managing common adrenal and pituitary disorders. Vincent was on the inpatient teaching service, hanging out with Dr. Coffman and some newly contracted physicians. Beatrice had been on another obstetrics rotation, on which she kept her comments brief.

"Bea, how have you been?" Vincent asked as he grabbed a large bottle of pinot noir and four wine glasses for the group. "I know you've had some challenging weeks on the OB service."

"It's been a long stretch, for sure," Beatrice answered with a strained grin. "I know we all go through rough patches in training, but this one has been particularly rough."

"I heard about the couplet that was rushed to the OR," Soraya said, scrunching her brow. "If you need to talk about any of that, please let me know because I can always make space and time to be there for you."

"I appreciate that."

Beatrice averted her gaze and nibbled on a cracker.

After filling everyone's glass with red wine, Vincent distributed them and proposed another toast—this time to our friendship and to making it through another month of residency training. As the night deepened, the tide rolled in with a soothing rhythm. I stood by the railing near the beach, looking out over the dark bay. The moonlight danced on the waves, each crest reflecting a world of possibilities. Soraya joined me, her presence a silent support. Seeing my colleagues and friends gathered together outside the sterility of the hospital and clinic filled me with a joy I had not felt in a long time.

"Who wants to head to the beach for a dance party?" Carmen, one of the first-year residents, yelled from back at the pergola. "I've got the tunes. Can I connect to the speaker?"

"Sure," Vincent answered, winding his way over to Carmen. "Let's get it set up and then head down to the beach."

Carmen and Vincent huddled near his Bluetooth speaker to connect her phone to it while I checked to see if Soraya and Beatrice wanted to go down and dance. Soraya enthusiastically accepted the invitation, whereas Beatrice indicated she wanted to "digest" a little before dancing. Within a few minutes, the portable speaker came to life with a pop hit from the 2010s. Vincent and Carmen threw their arms up wildly, preparing the partygoers to bust a move on the sand.

The moon hung low over the gently lapping waves, casting a silver glow on our makeshift dance floor. The day had faded into one of those rare, magical nights when the boundaries between colleagues softened. This spontaneous retreat was a much-needed escape from the grueling hours at our places of work. Vincent, Soraya, and I flung sand beneath our feet as we executed moves ranging from jubilant jumps to shameless dance routines. Now and then, my eyes darted back to the pergola, where Beatrice remained. Usually an active participant at any gathering, her subdued aura tonight was noticeable. A few partners of our co-residents surrounded her. Although they were engaged in conversation, Beatrice was visibly more reserved than usual. Vincent followed my gaze to where Beatrice was sitting.

"She's been sitting and chatting there for a long time," he said, his voice barely audible over the pulsating beats. "Maybe she's not feeling the dance floor tonight?"

Soraya, twirling with the rhythm, shrugged lightly.

"We should bring her dessert. A treat might cheer her up!"

I nodded, swallowing a pang of concern. Beatrice, one of my closest confidants in the chaotic whirlwind of residency, had been my rock. Seeing her isolated like this, even willingly, felt unsettling. As the music eventually quieted and people's laughter dimmed slightly from exhaustion, we made our way back to the pergola. Several of our co-residents had outdone themselves with desserts—trays laden with chocolate éclairs, mini cheesecakes, and fruit tarts glistened under the fairy lights. As we approached, Beatrice looked up and managed a warm yet clearly forced smile.

"You guys look like you had fun out there," she noted, observing the sand on our clothes.

"We missed you," I said, handing her a dessert plate. "Especially during that mash-up. You and your dance moves were sorely missed."

She chuckled, accepting the plate.

"I guess I just needed a slower pace tonight. Just feeling a little off. But I loved watching you all."

We sat beside her while Vincent handed out desserts to the others. The conversation gently turned to anecdotes from our day-to-day hustle at the hospital, the lighter cases, and whimsical thoughts of future endeavors beyond residency. Soraya gently nudged the conversation deeper, her voice soft but direct.

"Anything you want to talk about, Bea? We're here, you know."

Beatrice paused, her fingers tracing the rim of her dessert plate.

"It's nothing. I'm just getting trapped in my head. There's nothing for you all to worry about."

As we listened to Beatrice speak, the night felt less like a detachment from reality and more like a reminder of the connections that sustain us through every hardship. It was also a reminder of how to succor friends in need. Later, as the party disbanded and the last song played—a soft, acoustic rendition that seemed to wrap the night in a gentle embrace—Beatrice stood near the railing overlooking the beach, finishing her glass of pinot noir at last. As a few people lingered to wrap up their conversations, I strode to the railing to check in with Beatrice.

"Did you have a good time?" I tenderly asked as I leaned against the metal railing next to her.

"I did. I'm sorry if it didn't seem that way. The food was delicious, and it was so nice to see everyone."

My intuition told me I needed to be silent and make space for her, so I nodded and looked in her direction.

"I'm finding it hard to be as present as I once was before moving out here to Frieden Bay," Beatrice said after a few moments. "I don't know if it's the place or what, but sometimes it's hard for me to understand what the hell is going on with healthcare out here."

"I can relate to that," I said considerately. "I sometimes find it hard to accept the world I know when my mind is locked on the world I used to know. It makes me feel like I have no control over the outcomes in my life and that powerful others are calling all the shots for me."

"Retaining every bit of control is so valuable," she stated before turning around and revealing tears welling up in her eyes. "No amount of reassurance or guidance from leadership is helpful—it all feels like one frustrating platitude or false hope after another. I mean, look at what happened to Calisto."

The cool night breeze gently brushed against our faces as Beatrice and I made our way down the uneven sandy path to the beach. The sound of the crashing waves played softly in the background, like nature's lullaby soothing the restless thoughts that I knew were swirling in Beatrice's mind. Beneath her composed exterior, I knew the insecurities that gnawed at her. As we settled on the cool sand, I popped open a can of lime-flavored hard seltzer and handed another to Beatrice. She managed a thank-you, her eyes fixed on the horizon. Beatrice sighed after a few moments of silence, her gaze lingering on the distant waves.

"I don't know," she started, her voice barely above a whisper. "I'm just... I feel like I'm constantly drowning. No matter how much I try, I'm always a step behind. The other day, I hesitated during a procedure I had done half a dozen times prior. It was only for a moment, but it could've caused harm to the patient."

She paused, her hands trembling somewhat as she clasped the can tighter.

"I'm so scared of making a mistake, of not knowing enough."

Listening closely, I placed my drink aside and turned toward her.

"Before I was born, my parents escaped poverty back in Italy to live in the United States," she mumbled, furiously kicking at the sand. "They wanted me to be successful and thrive in this country. Become a doctor. Do great things. Look at me! I'm incompetent. A joke."

"Bea, being unsure doesn't mean you're incompetent. Every physician faces uncertainty. It's okay to feel afraid and anxious; it means you care, you know? What matters is how you handle those emotions and learn from them."

Beatrice looked at me, her eyes reflecting the moonlight and a palpable vulnerability.

"But, how do you deal with the fear of not being good enough?"

I thought for a moment before replying.

"By remembering your reason for starting this journey. Focus on the lives you've touched, the patients who've thanked you. Let that drive you."

She nodded slowly, taking a deep breath as she pondered my words.

"I know you're right. It's so hard to see the forest for the trees when you're so deep in it. However, if I close my eyes and concentrate, the smiles and looks of relief come into view."

"You are not alone in feeling like an impostor," I said hesitantly, scooting my bare feet across the smooth sand. "I first experienced that when we sat together on Dr. Altamura's boat during intern year. Do you remember the "dangers of double diuretics" lecture I got from Dr. Coffman when we were interns?"

Beatrice bobbed her head more animatedly, quietly chuckling. In my mind, I could hear my voice echoing disparagements about how ineffective I was as a physician. I closed my eyes tightly and suppressed the thoughts to return to the conversation with Beatrice.

"He gave you so much grief after you suggested starting an older man on two thiazide diuretics for hypertension. But that was an honest mistake."

"Still," I admitted, looking deeply into Beatrice's dark brown eyes. "I felt like a fraud for two weeks after that. Slowly, I regained my confidence in making the right patient care decisions. I will never fully understand what you specifically are experiencing, but that doesn't mean I can't relate to experiencing impostor syndrome."

Beatrice's smile widened as my words sunk in, giving her a brief respite from her inner critic.

"Thank you for that."

We continued discussing her experiences: the tough and rewarding days at the hospital. Eventually, the conversation drifted to lighter topics—old college memories and plans for the future. The tension in her posture eased as laughter mingled with the sounds of the sea. By the time we decided to head back, the moon had climbed higher in the sky, casting long shadows on the sand. As I walked her back to her apartment, I could sense a subtle shift in her demeanor—a lightness that had not been there earlier in the evening.

"Thank you again for everything: for listening and for the push," she turned to me, a small smile playing on her lips. "I think I just need some space for a little while to get back into a happier and healthier headspace."

"It's what friends are for," I replied with a grin.

She hugged me goodbye: a firm, grateful embrace. As I watched her disappear into her apartment, I felt a quiet hope for her. Beatrice was a fighter; I knew she would find her way. Calling for my ride, I glanced back at the moonlit path from her apartment to the beach, thinking about life's unpredictable tides and how our roles in people's lives change with the passage of time.

CHAPTER FOURTEEN

Paradise Lost

> *The fool's grave misstep is that it believes it is immune to the prevailing laws of nature, thinking that energy is infinite and ever accessible.*

Beatrice's words during our chat on the beach and walk back to her apartment left me with many questions and enough concern that I made efforts throughout the day to catch her in the clinic. Day after day, my attempts to converse with her resulted in me glimpsing her braided brown hair as it disappeared behind the scratched-up front door of the Primary Care Center. I did not think she was not specifically angry or upset with me. However, her uncharacteristic detachment from socializing and the absence of her usual morning pleasantries rendered me ill at ease. From a distance, I sensed that the recent changes in her life exceeded her capacity for resilience. As I saw my patients in the clinic, images of Beatrice's dejected face after our dinner a couple of weeks ago kept popping into my head.

Even my attempts to communicate with her remotely over text messages resulted in unrevealing and terse responses or complete radio silence for days at a time. It felt like an arrow going through my heart when I saw one-word responses where her natural speech pattern would normally be bubbly. Although I wanted to connect with her and raise her spirits, I decided it was best to respect her boundaries and give her every opening to approach me. It made me feel like a miserable failure as a colleague and friend for not being more persistent and delivering peace to her. I spent many long moments in my car in quiet contemplation about what I should do, my heart heavy from feeling weak and powerless. Fortunately, the quotidian routine of residency kept me moving—literally and figuratively—from one room to the next, mitigating my concerns one hour at a time.

The following Monday, I emerged from my car, clutching an iced coffee as if carrying my newborn child. Vincent's smiling face entered my line of sight abruptly as I processed the scenery just a few inches away from my person.

"I heard you had a cool case of bullous pemphigoid last week."

"That was an interesting one. I'm hopeful treating that lady will get her good results before the end of the month," I commented as I reached out to shake his hand. "How's everything at home?"

"Good, good," he replied as his receding smile signaled an impending change in subject. "I've been meaning to chat with you about Bea. It's been hard to talk with her recently. I've been thinking about the party the other week. I wonder if something I said upset her. Have you had any luck chatting with her?"

I tightened my lips in empathy with Vincent before shaking my head.

"It's been the same for me. I'm worried about Bea, but it doesn't seem fair to her to try to smother her if she isn't ready to reach out. We're a small and tight-knit group, so it's much harder to ignore someone who's not doing well."

"Exactly. I hope she's doing okay," he uttered before fixing his eyes on the coastline in the distance. "I overheard Dr. Mose discussing her recent clinical performance with Dr. Coffman. It didn't sound good. I haven't noticed it since we're in the clinic on different days now, but apparently, she's been canceling her sessions more and more frequently without giving much of a heads-up. I don't want that to result in a reprimand or anything like that."

The spreading tension from my lips caused my jaw to tighten on both sides as I considered the implications of what our Program Director and Associate Program Director were observing and discussing behind closed doors.

"That's concerning, for sure. I really hope I run into her soon. She is too good of a physician for anything to threaten her progress forward."

Vincent firmly patted my upper back, showing his agreement.

"Let's get inside and take care of some people. We can talk more later."

Feeling melancholy, we entered the Primary Care Center and checked in with our medical assistants before starting the workday. Despite the joyous moments of following up with a gentleman who had finally improved his average blood glucose levels after years of struggle and a young child now on a normal growth trajectory after being born small for gestational age, the small reminders of the unknowns surrounding Beatrice continually punctuated my joy. Perhaps the most distracting thing was that she was not at work today despite being on the schedule. Presumably, she had called out again, which made my stomach drop.

With the weather now comfortably warm in late June, I opted for a stroll through Dolphin Park after I arrived back at my apartment. Since getting back and dropping my stuff off, dense white clouds had accumulated in the sky, filtering and softening the light before it scattered across the trimmed grass and thriving trees and flowers covering most of the gathering place near my apartment complex. It was tranquil, and I put my headphones on to play some gentle music before taking off on my picturesque walk.

My eyelids relaxed as I mindfully attended to the rhythmic sound of drums emitting from my headphones. The evening air was a perfect temperature, creating the sensation of walking through nothing in an ethereal space. I took deep breaths in sync with the music and adjusted my stride to keep time with the drums. After a demanding day, decompressing like this felt second to none, and for several seconds, I allowed my vision to go out of focus to be entirely present in the moment.

As my eyes refocused, I saw Beatrice walking in the opposite direction along the path ahead of me. My heart raced at the sight of her because I had not had an opportunity to talk with her like this in what seemed like forever. I vigorously waved to her, and she raised her arm and reciprocated the gesture, trying but failing to match my energy.

Excitedly jogging up to her, I gave her a hug. She familiarly embraced me, reassuring me that my friend was still there.

"Bea, it's great to see you!"

"You, too," she said earnestly. "Do you want to sit down and talk?"

We made our way over to a rusted bench facing the water. Twilight was taking over, casting a vermillion glow over the park and producing a final warmth for this day now ending. The loud chattering and crowing of seagulls echoed across the park, and the sweet scent of a nearby flowerbed overpowered the smell of the saltwater.

"I'm sorry I haven't spoken to you in a while," Beatrice quietly stated with her contrition on full display. "It's been a rough few months, which I realize you already know."

Beneath her warm and comforting voice, Beatrice did not seem like herself; she seemed distant, lost even. Her typically bright eyes concealed a personal darkness that was altogether foreign.

"Has anything changed in the past few weeks?"

She paused for a moment before simply shrugging in response.

"Not in any positive way, unfortunately. I've been a pretty crappy resident lately..."

Her voice cracked as her eyes welled up with tears. As she tried hard to force her tears back, I started to understand much more about what had been happening at work and what had prompted her reclusive behavior.

"Have you been in touch with Mose and Coffman?" I inquired.

She hesitated momentarily before nodding, wordlessly acknowledging an unarticulated awareness of her situation.

"Yeah," she responded half-heartedly, uninterested in discussing it further.

We sat silently for about a minute to allow some mounting tension to dissipate before proceeding.

"How can we support you?" I gently probed to see if she would open up to me more. "You know, I've always looked up to you for how impressive you are as a physician, and none of that has changed."

After a few more moments of silence, Beatrice finally spoke. She talked about the stress she had been under in the hospital and clinic, the pressure to meet deadlines for the program and her patients, and the constant criticism she perceived from many people. She opened up about feeling burnt out and like her support system was withering. Beatrice made it clear that she—a veritable paragon of our specialty—felt like a failure.

I reached out and held her hand, a silent gesture of support. Beatrice tightly squeezed my hand, seemingly grateful. We sat quietly, her words heavy in the air around us.

"You know you're not alone, right?" I asked earnestly. "We are here for you. Whatever is going on is navigable; you will get past this. We believe in you. I mean, you'll be our new Chief in just a few days. That's a vote of confidence like no other."

Beatrice's shoulders relaxed at my words, and a faint smile spread over her lips. I noticed a small but unmistakable scar on her lower lip. Had she had an injury? Maybe an accident while riding her bike?

As the deep violet of the evening took over the sky, we exchanged stories from when we first met and laughed together, baring our souls to each other. It was a cathartic experience, a much-needed moment of connection between two friends who had lost touch. Once it had become completely dark, we stood to leave, feeling lighter and more connected than we had in quite some time. As we walked back along the path, the darkness that had shrouded Beatrice seemed to lift somewhat, replaced by hope and renewal. Beatrice hugged me tightly, thanking me for being there for her. After I helped her get back to her apartment, we said our goodbyes, and she said she would see me at work tomorrow.

I walked into the clinic in the morning and caught a beautiful sight: Beatrice laughing and joking with Soraya and one of the interns. I grinned and chuckled as I went to my desk to prepare a mug of green tea and review my patients' charts. I reached over to the small copper watering can in the workroom and sprinkled some water on the pothos sitting atop my overhead storage bin. In many respects, this morning felt like any other, and that was uplifting for me.

Like a freight train pulling up to a depot, the swift clopping of Dr. Mose's boots could be heard echoing from the hallway leading into the resident workroom.

"Dr. Portinari," Dr. Mose said calmly as she approached Beatrice. "Could you come with me to my office?"

From across the room, I saw Beatrice's demeanor flatten as she followed closely behind Dr. Mose. I shuddered at the suddenness of the interaction before returning to my morning preparations. After fifteen minutes, I heard Beatrice's slow steps returning to the workroom. She was breathing heavily, which alerted me to something being amiss.

Beatrice's face showed panic and desperation as she trudged back to where I was sitting. She sullenly approached me and took a seat next to my desk.

"I don't know what to do," she whispered hoarsely, becoming increasingly lachrymose with each word. "I'm lost; I'm scared."

"What happened?" I asked in a hushed voice. "What did Dr. Mose say?"

"She's suspending me based on my recent performance," she muttered. "This is not the first conversation we've had about this possibility. She and Coffman really tried for me. What do I do? I can't work somewhere else. My life is over."

Mouth agape, I gazed at Beatrice, unable to process what she was saying.

"We'll see any patients on your schedule that need to be seen today. I have some openings. Tonight, let's talk more, okay?"

Beatrice nodded disconsolately and rose quickly from the chair she was sitting in. As she left the building, I sighed heavily and closed my eyes, contemplating what I would say this evening. I cleared my mind and re-centered on what I needed to accomplish today.

Once my last patient checked out, I collected my laptop bag and other belongings before rushing outside to drive over to Beatrice's apartment. I kept the radio on at a low volume while rehearsing a few scenarios. I would feel distraught and lost if I were in her position. The pain etched into her face earlier was difficult to witness, especially in someone so exceptional at providing healthcare.

Once parked in her complex, I immediately marched up to her apartment. I knocked on her door and noticed something out of the ordinary: the door was left ajar and opened farther in response to my knuckles making contact. I carefully entered her apartment, unsure what I would find on the inside.

Her apartment was unusually quiet: no whirring of her oscillating fans or droning of a song on her stereo in her room. The pervasive silence was strange, even for Beatrice and her reserved tendencies. I strode down the hallway from the foyer to the living room and came across an old end table with her wallet on top of it. I scoped out the other rooms of her apartment and found no one else inside. Thankfully, nothing seemed out of place or stolen.

"Bea?" I called out across the apartment. "Bea? It's me. I just got here and found the door open. Is everything okay?"

No answer. I tried calling her phone to no avail. I could not hear the phone's vibration somewhere else in the apartment. I rubbed my face in confusion before writing a little note to Beatrice on her refrigerator and then headed back outside, firmly pulling the door shut. Seeing her wallet in the living room made me think she was probably sitting outside, which she would sometimes do in the evenings when the weather was nice.

Heading down the stairs from the second floor, I turned the corner and caught a glimpse of the dark blue of her car, which sat well positioned in its normal parking spot. I excitedly ran to the car, gesturing in line with the front windshield to get Beatrice's attention. As I approached the vehicle, the silhouette of a lone occupant in the driver's seat became visible. It must have been her sitting there. Who else would it be?

The occupant was as static as a statue, holding the same position as if in a deep slumber. I stepped closer to see the faint outline of Beatrice's countenance, which provoked fear deep within me.

What was it about her that did not seem right?

I paused for a moment to observe more closely. Her eyes were closed.

Was she sleeping in her car? But why would she do that if she could sleep in her bed?

Her mouth was slightly open as if she were breathing through it. Her makeup was smudged, with streaks of black mascara coating her cheeks. She must have been crying for a while. Then, I saw that scar on her lower lip again.

How did that happen?

I knocked on the driver's side front window and said her name. No response. Not even a muscle twitch. Something about the situation caused the arrector pili muscles all across my body to fire.

It was at that moment I saw something that caused my chest to tighten: small blue pills littering the passenger seat and a crumpled piece of aluminum foil sitting adjacent to them. A transient paralysis overtook my body. I stood in the same spot for what felt like an eternity—without motion, speech, or thought. My mind became a white, immense void with speckles of indiscernible color emerging deep within it.

Another thing caught my eye: the glint of a long, cylindrical piece of glass sitting in one of the cupholders. My conscious mind was failing me, but the gears of my subconscious world were rotating with a fierce velocity. I turned my attention back to the scar on her lip and felt something click in my head.

Where had I seen that before?

I racked my brain to clarify this moment of déjà vu. A face popped into my mind, bearing the same scar.

Claire...

Despite being without my faculties, my arms started to move. I felt myself lurch toward the driver's side door. When the door handle did not budge, I threw down my bag and removed my jacket before wrapping it hastily around my right elbow. Before I knew it, small splinters formed on the window, but my shielded elbow failed to go through the glass. I hurriedly located a rock and finished the job. After smashing the window, I urgently unlocked the door and opened it.

"Bea? Bea! Say something!" I yelled at her, trying in vain to get her attention. "I need help over here!"

I shook her forcefully by the shoulders to elicit a response. I pushed up on her eyelids and shone my penlight into her pupils. It was indisputable: the pinpoint pupils spoke to the toxicity decreasing her consciousness. I ripped the seat belt off of her so I could remove her from the vehicle and more appropriately assess the situation.

By this point, several neighbors had gathered near the vehicle, gasping in horror as I dragged her limp body onto the pavement.

"I need you to call 911 right away," I calmly told a middle-aged woman standing closest to us. "Tell me once you know the ambulance is on the way."

I quickly looked down at Beatrice and buried my knuckles into her sternum to see if I could get her to respond to a painful stimulus. Nothing. At the same time, I noted that her chest was rising and falling, but her respiratory rate was dangerously low. I placed my index and middle fingers over her carotid artery and was able to palpate a weak pulse. Without even thinking about it, I pulled my laptop bag toward me and removed a new container of naloxone nasal spray I had in it.

"They'll be here in two minutes," the woman reported as I continued the resuscitation.

With my years of medical training guiding my body, I administered the naloxone into each nostril before casting aside the used medication.

"Sir," I pointed directly at a man standing nearby with his hand over his mouth. "Come here and help me reposition her."

He made his way to Beatrice's opposite side. I instructed him on how to put her in a recovery position while the naloxone took effect. We supported her head, flexed her right knee, and then rolled her onto her left side. Beatrice continued to breathe in a shallow and slow pattern, and her central pulses remained intact.

The next series of events flew by me in a blur of activity I could barely process. Once the paramedics arrived, I blurted out the interventions we had done for a good handoff, and then they quickly took over and loaded her into the truck. I accepted the offer to ride up front while we sped off to Alta Vista Hospital. As the ambulance sailed through the local streets with its siren blaring and lights pulsing, I stared down at the dashboard, noticing that my surroundings were becoming fuzzy with an odd distortion. It was almost as if I were traveling through a fog that others could not see.

When we arrived, the paramedics rapidly transitioned Beatrice to the emergency department team. On the gurney, Beatrice appeared even more like a statue than she had in her car, which sent a debilitating chill down my spine. During this handoff, I overheard the paramedics' findings from the back of the rig, all of which made my skin crawl: low heart rate, hypotension, low respiratory rate, hypoxia, one dose of naloxone in the field and another en route. This was very bad, and I knew it. On our way over, an intravenous line had been started, with a bolus of normal saline now running.

I followed behind closely while Beatrice was expeditiously moved to a giant resuscitation bay, where her comatose body was transferred onto a bed from the gurney. Looking on in horror from outside of the resuscitation bay, I watched closely as a resident physician, her attending physician, and three nurses flooded into the room to continue resuscitating Beatrice. Although I wanted to help and bring my dear friend back from this, I knew I was far too compromised and needed to stay out of the way. In a matter of two minutes, Beatrice's condition deteriorated: she became apneic, and her other vital signs worsened in conjunction with the respiratory arrest.

Bea, breathe! Please breathe! I thought, noticing the fuzziness of the emergency department increasing like snow on an old television screen.

"Get our pharmacist in the room," the attending shouted over the noise. "We need to do a rapid-sequence intubation."

I felt tears stream down my face as I realized what was likely going to transpire here in spite of everyone's best efforts. The room exploded with activity, erupting into a cacophony as the physicians and nurses recognized the patient before them. For a split second frozen in time, I looked around and saw a dozen people doing different things to save Beatrice: the on-call pharmacist pushing a cart of sedatives, anesthesia induction agents, and neuromuscular blockers; a respiratory therapist setting up a mechanical ventilator for the eventual intubation; three nurses and the attending working on repositioning the patient; the resident preparing a metal laryngoscope blade for the intubation at the head of the bed; two nurses collecting various supplies and medications for the procedure; and three other staff members on standby, awaiting instructions on how to facilitate everything taking place. Observing all of this at once was surreal and made my head pound.

I watched as the endotracheal tube went down her throat and as the ventilatory bag was attached. Meanwhile, the respiratory therapist continued to set up the ventilator. I saw the cardiac monitor turn red and shriek as a clear stretch of ventricular fibrillation took over the display. Petrified, I watched the team call the code, grab the crash cart, and defibrillate her multiple times before she became asystolic. I then watched the multiple rounds of chest compressions and multiple administrations of epinephrine. All during this, I watched Beatrice's pale, unresponsive, and lifeless body lying motionless on the bed, intimating the truth that none of us wanted to accept.

"We have to call it now," the resident announced, weeping as she did. "Everyone, stop what you're doing. Let's come together for a moment."

I could not believe it, even though I witnessed everything with my eyes. Dr. Beatrice Portinari was gone. Time of death: 9:03 pm. I covered my head with my hands and slowly slid down against the wall to the floor, where I sat and cried loudly. I had an out-of-body experience where I felt myself floating above my physical body, head down against my knees.

What am I going to do without her? I thought, hovering in that higher space. *She was so strong. I am not nearly the physician she was.*

A hand on my left shoulder snapped me back into my body. Lifting my head, I then saw the emergency medicine resident crouched down near me, clearly shaken by all that had occurred.

"My name is Dr. Alexandra Quintana," she introduced herself with equanimity. "Let's get you to a safe and quiet room where we can talk, okay?"

"Okay," I managed to utter as I grabbed her outstretched hand to stand up.

As I followed her to a more secluded hallway within the unit, I took one last look at the resuscitation bay, where I saw two distraught nurses removing sensors from Beatrice's body.

Bea... I thought. *You can't be gone. Not you, too.*

CHAPTER FIFTEEN

Ashes

> *However, as one would expect, the fool is left as barren as an arid desert, without the vitality that makes life rich and worth the effort.*

I sat at an easel in a musty and dim studio, using my palette knife to blend two oil paints. Although I did not remember receiving formal training in painting, something about holding a brush felt natural. As I started working on my new creation, a door slammed open on the other side of the room, casting a sinister light across my canvas.

"What sort of person do you take yourself for?" Beatrice challenged as she stomped in my direction. "You're disgraceful, wasting your life away in this crappy hellhole that people call Frieden Bay and painting these worthless caricatures of an insipid ship scene. Pathetic! What exactly are you hoping to accomplish by the end of this hopeless mission? Dignity? Glory? It amazes me that you haven't figured it out yet."

From behind a tattered canvas, I held my gaze steady, the bristles of my brush dripping phthalo blue onto a stained drop cloth beneath my stool. Her words, harsh like the winds of winter, were cruel and cold. Yet, I found a strange energy bubbling beneath the surface—not indignation or resentment, but a blossoming resolve.

"I see things differently, Beatrice," I finally replied, my voice steady. "The norms of this town have suffocated me for far too long. This is my chance to turn over a new leaf and show what I can really contribute to our culture."

Nestled on a rocky inlet, Frieden Bay was a weathered remnant of the past, untouched by the rush of modernity that swept through metropolises like a blazing fire. It was here, amidst the constant whispers of the Frieden Sea and the relentless bullying of the wind and waves, that I found my retreat—my refuge. I saw life not in the hustle for wealth or fame but in the quiet moments of nature's untampered beauty, which I captured on my canvases.

"You wouldn't understand," I continued, glancing briefly at the unfinished sketch of the old ship.

The Albatross was a vessel that had traversed seas unknown and witnessed the world beyond our imaginations but now rested—weary and forgotten—in the arms of Frieden Bay. Its captain had met an untimely demise at the hands of a cruel fate. This ship was a symbol—not of decay but of a proud, subdued resilience. It represented a transcendence that only someone called Ishmael had embodied before.

How could you? I lamented to myself.

This was not just about painting. It was about perception, about seeing value in what others deemed worthless. I dipped my brush into my ochre paint, the ship's rusted hues demanding to be immortalized in this piece. I focused on capturing the fine details of the hull before tending to the other sections of the ship.

Beatrice scoffed, pacing with a frayed elegance around the cramped space of my studio, cluttered with easels and stained with the ghosts of colors past.

"Art is about expression, yes," she initiated, unable to conceal her aversion, "but it's also about communication. Who in this small town of Frieden Bay cares about an old ship that sank so long ago? This is a dying town, for crying out loud."

"That's why," I protested, my voice rising with a passion I seldom allowed myself to reveal. "Art is about life, about recording history and emotion and the very soul of a place before it's swallowed by time."

She regarded me then with confusion and curiosity as if seeing me for the first time.

"Do you really believe you'll change anything with these… pictures?"

"Not change," I murmured, a gentle smile tugging at the corners of my lips, contrasting the fury I had harbored moments ago. "Remember: I paint so that perhaps one day someone will look at these 'pictures' and remember Frieden Bay not as a crappy hellhole but as a place that held beauty, stories, and lives worth noting. To never forget the great ones who gave us the opportunities we have today."

Beatrice fell silent then, her eyes wandering to the canvas, to the bold strokes and vibrant colors that brought *The Albatross* back to life under my fervent hands. Minutes stretched into an eternity of silent understanding or perhaps acceptance. Finally, she spoke, her voice softer and hesitant.

"Maybe I was too harsh. This ship, your art. Maybe they do mean something."

My hand paused with brush mid-air, and my heart thundered with the validation I never knew I needed.

"They do, Beatrice. To me, they mean everything."

As she left, the door creaked softly, closing with a whisper that seemed to echo through the room, filling it with a new purpose. I returned to the canvas with my resolve solidified by confrontation. However, as I sauntered over to retrieve some more tubes of pigment from a cabinet in my study, an acrid smell assaulted my nose. I whipped around and screamed in horror as I saw titanic flames shoot up like a geyser from the floor, enveloping my canvas in a kiss of death. I frantically filled a basin with water and hurled it at the flames, only to be mocked by the subsequent puff of steam and a hellish cackling emanating from the giant chasm that formed on the floor. I peered into the abyss and stood aghast as I saw the tormented faces of Beatrice and Dr. Altamura staring back at me, reaching out to pull me down.

I sat heavily in the soft, worn armchair opposite Dr. Price. Her office was a small, cozy room with shelves full of books and certificates adorning the walls. The air smelled faintly of lavender, which sadly did little to calm my fraught nerves today.

"How often are you having these nightmares about Beatrice and Dr. Altamura?" Dr. Price asked, leaning in empathically. "I cannot imagine how troubling these must be for you."

"Yeah," I muttered with my arms crossed defensively. "Ever since she died, it has been awful. Every night, I have nightmares about fighting with her or the events before her death. Every day, I have flashbacks and re-experience the trauma. Occasionally, like the one last night, Dr. Altamura gets pulled into the whirlpool of these cursed dreams."

Dr. Price nodded slowly, her face a mask of concern.

"Can you tell me about these nightmares? It might help to talk through them."

I hesitated, rubbing my forehead as if I could wipe away the images that haunted me. Finally, I started speaking in a low, halting voice.

"In the dreams, it's always dark, whether we are inside or outside. We're arguing about something trivial, which was not like us before she died. But in the nightmare, it escalates. She's yelling, and I'm yelling back, and then…" I paused, swallowing hard, "…then it shifts. We're at her apartment complex where she… where it happened."

"Go on," Dr. Price encouraged softly.

"I try to resuscitate her just like I did in real life. But I always slip when I reach out to grab her so I can remove her from the vehicle. Then I'm helplessly watching as she either bursts into flames, dies in the emergency department, or cries out for help from me. Then I wake up, often drenched in sweat with the worst palpitations I have ever experienced."

"Those dreams sound incredibly vivid and distressing," Dr. Price observed. "It's a clear sign of unresolved guilt and trauma. It might help to develop more outlets to explore what you are feeling and experiencing. Sometimes, creative expression helps diminish trauma's power over us."

"I'm not sure I'm ready for that," I confessed, feeling a combination of fear and fatigue.

I felt an ache in my chest—a profound sorrow—knowing that Beatrice was gone and nothing could bring her back. I also felt guilty.

What could I have done differently?

Why didn't I see this coming?

"That's perfectly understandable," she reassured. "We can take small steps. Perhaps start by talking more about Beatrice and the good memories you shared. Focusing on the positive might help balance your perception and decrease the intensity of the nightmares."

Her suggestion was sound, grounded in her years of expertise in dealing with grief. We also discussed starting prazosin for my nightmares to see if it could decrease their intensity and frequency. I happily accepted the prescription before leaving the office.

After the session with Dr. Price, I was tangled in thoughts as I drove home. The sky was transitioning from dusky pinks to a deep velvet blue, somehow mirroring the flux of my own emotions as I mulled over the disaster of Beatrice's untimely departure and my conversation with Alexandra Quintana in the sterile chill of the emergency department.

Despite being only a second-year emergency medicine resident, Alexandra handled our meeting with a poise that belied her years. We sat in a secluded, softly lit consultation room—the atmosphere somber and heavy with unsaid words. She offered her professional condolences with a sincerity that reached her eyes—a rarity in the exhausting carousel of shifts in a place where burnout and demoralization often ran amok.

"I want to acknowledge the tremendous pain and loss this was for you," she began, her voice steady and reflecting practiced composure. "Beatrice was not just a colleague but a friend to many, and her contributions to this hospital were invaluable."

I nodded, the lump in my throat thick. It was hard to focus on Alexandra's words, and my mind replayed the countless hours Beatrice and I had spent together, both on grueling night shifts and in celebratory moments.

"From what we have gathered so far," Alexandra continued tactfully, "it appears that Beatrice's condition escalated due to acute respiratory failure, which might have been due to xylazine-contaminated fentanyl since she did not respond to the naloxone we gave her. Our toxicology panel is still pending further analysis to understand more about what happened in this case."

As physicians, we were both all too familiar with the academic side of drug interactions and overdose management, but facing this reality as colleagues and friends was something altogether different. It was raw. It was visceral. It was unbelievably traumatic. Alexandra's eyes met mine, clear and firm.

"I know this must be hard to process, especially considering your close relationship with her. We are here if you need anything more—any questions or support."

I swallowed, eventually finding my voice.

"Thank you, Alexandra. I... I just need some time to process this."

"Of course. Please take all the time you need. We're compiling a full report, and I'll make sure you receive all the necessary information. It's critical we all understand how we could prevent these tragedies in the future," she assured me, her tone a mix of compassion and professionalism.

As I pulled into my driveway, the heaviness of the day's revelations hung over me like a dark cloud. The apartment was almost too quiet as I let myself in. I tossed my keys on the dining room table and slumped into the couch, the echoes of my conversation with Alexandra replaying in my mind. Later that evening, as I sat there with my thoughts, I took out my journal. Writing had always been my haven in the chaos of life. I started to write down everything about Beatrice—her piercing intelligence, tireless dedication, leadership, and how much she meant to everyone at the hospital and clinic. I knew these would be the words I would say at her funeral. Through scratching a ballpoint pen against paper, I also noted everything I learned from the events leading to her death, seeing if something could have been different.

As I pulled up to the church in Beatrice's hometown, I espied Lorenzo and Isabella, Beatrice's parents whom I had met once before when we first started residency. They stood on the sidewalk in front of the house of worship conversing while Fernando, Beatrice's younger brother, listlessly came down the stairs leading up to the portico of the church. I sighed heavily, mentally preparing myself for Beatrice's funeral. I walked up to Lorenzo, Isabella, and Fernando and offered my condolences. They expressed how grateful they were to have me there and for everything I did to help Beatrice. As we entered the church together, a magnificent cerulean urn rested on the dais where the minister was setting up for the service.

As the urn glinted under the soft light filtering through the stained-glass windows, I could feel the heaviness of the day settling over me, causing my neck to ache from the muscle tension. Beatrice, with her enthusiastic smiles and ceaseless curiosity, had been more than just a co-resident in our program; she had been a vibrant spirit whose presence was irreplaceable. She was my friend and the greatest person I had ever met. Today, we gathered in this solemn sanctuary to say our final farewells.

Lorenzo clasped my hand with a strength that belied his grief.

"Thank you for coming," he reiterated, his voice marked by a feathery tremor of sorrow.

"It's the least I could do," I replied, managing a weak smile.

Isabella embraced me tightly, her body trembling with sobs.

"We know how much you meant to each other. Seeing you here helps a little," she whispered, her words muffled against my shoulder.

I simply nodded, not trusting my voice.

The three of us turned as Fernando approached, his steps slow and his eyes downcast, both of which exuded a somberness that made him appear older than his nineteen years.

"Hey there, Fernando," I said, touching his shoulder.

He looked up, offering a brief, pained smile before quickly looking away.

"Hi," he replied softly and laconically.

The rows of wooden pews were filled with faces, some familiar, others strangers, all united in mourning. Photographs of Beatrice from different stages of her life adorned one side of the aisle: her graduation, our residency group photo, and several of her adventurous trips; her face always alighted with fearless excitement. On the dais with her urn stood an easel bearing a large headshot she had taken while still a medical student and a gorgeous standing spray filled with roses, peace lilies, and other flowers she held near and dear. Vincent made his presence known and brought over Soraya and Ibrahim, her husband. We hugged each other with doleful expressions, barely masking the river of tears in each of our eyes.

We took our seats as the minister began the service, his voice soothing yet sorrowful. The solemn yet assuasive scent of patchouli incense filled the church. Its stained-glass windows fragmented the light into a spectrum of hues, casting a celestial pattern upon the congregation as if blessing each member individually. The pews, aged yet sturdy, cradled the grieving as they listened to Reverend Lyle's compassionate voice.

"Thank you all for joining us today," Reverend Lyle started, his voice—warm yet tinted with grief—resonating against the rafters. "It is always a sad day when we must say goodbye to someone who has left this world. Today, we are here to say goodbye to Dr. Beatrice Portinari, a young physician training in family medicine in Frieden Bay."

The ripple of weeping grew louder at the mention of her name. Every heart in the church was heavy, every eye wet. The loss was palpable, as tangible as the wooden pews on which we sat.

"She has left this world, destined to join our Lord in Heaven," Reverend Lyle continued, guiding us through the painful grief. "She has left behind her loving family and friends as well as a beautiful legacy: the improvements to our community through her work in healthcare."

As the service proceeded, various people close to Beatrice approached the lectern. Her mother recounted tales of Beatrice's youth, spirited and ambitious even as a child. Her father spoke of her ceaseless compassion for those who suffered and told a story of her medical mission work in college and medical school. Her brother recalled her bright laughter echoing through their home and the silly fights they would have, always ending in laughter. Her friends shared memories of her relentless pursuit of improving patient care, of late-night study sessions, and of her dreams to change the world.

Then, it was my turn. I walked up to the lectern, a deep breath steadying my quivering hands. I looked out at the mournful eyes of the congregation, feeling the immense pressure of the task before me. Beatrice was not just a friend and co-resident; she was a beacon of hope, a relentless force in healthcare, and a cherished companion.

"Good morning, everyone," I began, my voice faltering with the potency of my emotions. "I had the distinct honor and privilege of working alongside Beatrice and calling her my friend. Beatrice was more than just a doctor; she was a visionary in her approach to family medicine. She saw each patient as a story, a life, a family: not just a set of symptoms to be treated."

I paused, recalling countless shifts beside her, witnessing her passion and determination.

"Beatrice often said that medicine was an art as much as a science. She painted her canvas with empathy, care, and exceptional skill, changing her patients' lives for the better. Even in the darkest moments, she was a light, both in and out of the hospital. She represented the heart and soul of our profession, and I always looked to her example to figure out how I could grow as a physician."

Looking down at my hands, I related a personal memory that had always stayed with me.

"One late night, after a particularly taxing shift, we sat in the physician's lounge at the hospital, and she confided in me that every patient she cared for nurtured her soul and that every patient lost was like an anchor around her neck. But she never let that weight slow her down. Instead, it drove her to fight harder, to learn more, and to always care deeply."

I breathed, scanning the sea of faces, finding fortitude in remembering her.

"Her legacy will not rest merely in our memories," I concluded. "Her legacy will live on in every life she touched, every person she healed, and every heart she warmed. Today, we mourn her absence and celebrate the profound impact she made upon us all. Beatrice may have left this world, but her spirit, her dreams, and her aspirations reside within each of us who knew her."

As I returned to my seat, the caring nods of agreement and the shared tears painted a clear picture: Beatrice's life, though tragically short, was undeniably meaningful. Vincent stood in the pew to embrace me tightly, overcome with his own emotions, while Soraya and Ibrahim grasped my hands in a small gesture of gratitude for my eulogy. Reverend Lyle resumed, offering pacifying words and prayers as we all bade our final earthly farewell to the remarkable Dr. Beatrice Portinari, who had departed too soon but left an indelible mark on the world and our hearts.

After the service, as people filed out to the graveyard for the burial, I lingered for a moment by the dais. The urn was beautiful, decorated with intricate patterns that seemed to dance in the light—a stark contrast to its purpose. This formal goodbye felt surreal, as if I half-expected Beatrice to walk through the doors, her laughter ringing out to shatter the silence.

"Are you okay?" Fernando's voice pulled me from my thoughts.

"Yeah," I lied, "Just remembering your sister."

"Me too," he said, looking toward the urn. "She talked about you a lot, you know. Said you made the crazy hours at the hospital and clinic bearable."

I chuckled softly, the warmth of a large tear pooling up in the corner of my eye.

"She did the same for me."

We left the church together, joining the other mourners at the graveyard where Beatrice would be laid to rest. The ceremony was short but powerful, and the moment finally arrived for the interment of Beatrice's ashes. As the urn was lowered into the ground, something snapped in my head: she was gone forever. My weak knees buckled, and I fell to the ground, sobbing at the finality of this moment. I would never see her again, never speak to her again, never embrace her again. Vincent knelt beside me, holding me close as he cried with me. Soraya placed a hand tenderly on my head as we grieved together.

CHAPTER SIXTEEN

The Dark Army

> *The fool's fundamental problem is that it lives vicariously and believes that the images presented to it in its mind represent actual experience. Much to its chagrin, there is no substitute for experiencing tribulation.*

The court was filled with the mellifluous sound of rustling leaves in autumn as servants scurried across the chamber, tending to the whims of the guests who spoke in inaudible voices. I sat there in a stupor, deeply ensconced in my throne. There, enveloped by the warmth of my busy court, I waited as the day unfolded with the anticipation of routine and prosperity. The faces around me were familiar. Conversations melded into a lulling hum, barely piercing the serene bubble of my kingdom.

One day, my trusted advisor broke the monotony, a slight furrow knitting his usually unflappable brow.

"Your Majesty, a messenger approaches with news that demands your audience," he cautioned with discreet urgency.

I signaled my understanding and gestured for the messenger to advance. A clang of armor announced the newcomer's approach, his visage concealed beneath a modest helm.

"Your Majesty," he bowed deeply, "a soothsayer of notable repute, Calchas by name, implores your grace to grant him an audience. He speaks of omens dire and critical."

Intrigue piqued, I assented, curiosity threading my voice.

"Let him enter."

The court's murmur dwindled to silence as a cloaked figure glided into the chamber. The soothsayer's presence charged the air with a palpable tension. With a deferential bow, the hooded Calchas addressed the assembly.

"Majesty, wisdom necessitates heed. Three specters of fate accompany me, each bearing prophecies you must not ignore."

As he spoke, shimmers of ethereal light coalesced into forms beside him: three specters, translucent and seemingly wrought from the cosmos. The first, a spectral knight cloaked in darkness, spoke with a booming voice that echoed like distant thunder.

"Beware Draconius, commander of the Dark Army, whose shadow longs to beleaguer your realm."

The second was a delicate spirit adorned with feathers, its voice as soft as the susurration of leaves.

"Only a bird of the same feather can smite you."

Lastly, the third, an apparition wrapped in verdant vines, its voice like the creak of ancient boughs.

"Your kingdom shall crumble if the woods encroach upon this court."

As the specters vanished, leaving behind a trail of chilling mist, the soothsayer bowed again.

"Heed these words, our most exalted King. Prepare and prevail, or hesitate and falter."

After the soothsayer withdrew, a pensive mood enveloped me. I had not before heard the utterance of Draconius' name, but the people of my kingdom had long told tales of the Dark Lord who would lead the Dark Army. His existence as a tangible threat seemed surreal. One thing I knew for certain was that denial would not dispel danger.

"The nightmares are getting worse," I said, observing a bird as it flew past the office window.

"What was the last dream or nightmare you remember having?"

I described the ominous dream of Calchas the Soothsayer visiting me in a distant kingdom, warning of my downfall through three spirits.

"That sounds very distressing," Dr. Price frowned, writing on her notepad. "Have you noticed any positive changes since we switched your medications?"

"Maybe a little bit," I shrugged. "The anxiety is still intense, and my mood issues have not improved as we had hoped they would."

Dr. Price nodded thoughtfully, scribbling a few more notes onto her notepad.

"It's important that we monitor this closely. Sometimes, the full effects of medication adjustments take a while to manifest. However, let's talk more about your nightmares. Do you think there's a pattern or specific triggers?"

I shifted uncomfortably in my seat, the leather squeaking softly under me.

"I'm not sure about a pattern, but recently, these dreams have featured a lurking danger that eventually arises and consumes me. It's as if my subconscious is staging an ancient drama as punishment for my wrongdoings."

"Interesting," Dr. Price murmured, her eyes reflecting curiosity. "This could be your mind's way of processing stress or fear through metaphorical narratives. Do these figures interact with you directly?"

"Yes. There's been a pattern of some figure conveying a message of doom or a moral lesson. It's like living through a fable every night."

Dr. Price leaned back, her fingers tapped lightly against the side of her chin.

"You've mentioned that you've enjoyed reading older books about historical and mythological topics. Could it be possible that your choice of reading is influencing your dreams?"

I pondered the suggestion.

"Possibly. But it feels deeper than that, as if these dreams are trying to tell me something about myself, something I might be missing."

"Let's explore that," Dr. Price proposed. "If we look at Calchas, he wasn't just a bearer of bad news but a guide through difficult truths. Maybe your subconscious is employing these characters to help you confront something. What do you think it might be guiding you toward?"

I took a deep breath, letting her words sink in. It was a novel perspective, but it resonated a bit too closely. Recently, my life felt as if it were at a crossroads, both in my career and my personal relationships. Fear of making the wrong decision might very well be manifesting through these heralds in my sleep.

"Lately, I've been avoiding making some big decisions," I admitted slowly. "Maybe my mind is using these figures to push me to confront these choices."

Dr. Price smiled slightly.

"Dreams can sometimes be our greatest advisors. Would you be open to trying some journaling about these dreams immediately after waking up? Writing could help externalize and clarify their meanings. It may also help with processing the posttraumatic stress, which I know is also affecting you significantly."

"I can try journaling," I said, relief washing over me.

I was happy to have a potential solution.

One morning, about two weeks after Beatrice's funeral, Soraya came into the resident workroom of the Primary

Care Center, her expression unmistakably glowing with innovation—the sort of expression that promised something interesting was about to unfold.

"I found this recipe online for paella, and given everything that we have been dealing with, we should make this together and enjoy a nice meal," she declared, her eyes gleaming.

Vincent and I exchanged a glance. Our mundane tasks—documentation, prior authorizations, and other clerical work—had been especially draining lately, and Soraya's suggestion was a lighthearted reprieve we both craved.

"I would love to do that," I responded, feeling a flutter of enthusiasm at the prospect of doing something out of the ordinary. "Would we do it at your place?"

"Yes," she replied, giddy with anticipation. "Why don't you all drop by next Friday? I'll get all of the ingredients. I would appreciate it if one of you could bring a dessert and the other some drinks."

Vincent, ever the enthusiast for sweet treats, volunteered for dessert, leaving me to ponder the drink selection. After closing the loop on our dinner plans, we parted ways to attend to our patient care responsibilities. Throughout my clinic sessions over the next week, I had some deeply touching interactions with my patients: an elderly woman who thanked me for getting insurance to cover her daily inhalers, a young man who expressed appreciation to me for my gender-inclusive care, and a mother who showed her gratitude with a fruit arrangement for admitting and caring for her baby girl in the hospital. It was a testament to what makes primary care the foundation of healthcare and why I love family medicine.

As Friday afternoon gave way to dusk, I found myself scrutinizing bottles at a local liquor store, finally selecting a Spanish sangria that would complement the rich, savory flavors of the paella. Meanwhile, Vincent messaged me a photo of an extravagant chocolate torte he picked up from the local bakery, and I chuckled at his classic and unapologetically decadent choice. Arriving at Soraya's townhouse, the ambrosial aromas of onions and garlic sizzling in a large iron skillet graced us. Soraya was orchestrating her kitchen like a maestro, her movements precise and graceful.

Vincent waltzed in with his torte, setting it on the counter with a flourish that earned an amused giggle from Soraya. I placed the sangria on the table alongside glasses that caught the evening moonlight, casting colorful reflections onto the white tablecloth. The simmering of the delicious rice dish in the skillet melded with the occasional clink of glasses and gave the kitchen the charm of a fancy Spanish restaurant. The three of us chopped, stirred, and laughed, each pitching in on the labor. The now golden paella promised a feast for all of us, but the kitchen's warmth nourished something beyond our stomachs.

Finally, as we settled around the table and served the amazing-looking paella, rich with seafood and spices, the first spoonfuls were met with approving murmurs and nods. The fruity and fresh sangria was the perfect accompaniment, matching the meal's flavors superbly. Vincent's chocolate torte was a grand finale when we thought the evening could not get any better. There was no doubt that our meal satisfied our gluttonous sides.

With our plates now empty, we turned to good conversation among friends. Inarguably, it was one of the most heartfelt meals we had experienced in a long time. We retreated to the garden in the front yard of the townhouse, relaxing on some red and white Adirondack chairs. Sitting there in the humid breeze of the twilight, the savory scent of the paella still wafting through the air, I could feel the tension inside of me slowly starting to loosen. It dawned on me that this was the first time we had gathered outside of work without Beatrice since the incident, which left me with a pang of sadness.

"Bea always talked about how gatherings like these refreshed her soul." Vincent was the first to open up, staring into the nearest lantern whose flame danced and flickered wistfully. "She always knew how to get us to spend time together meaningfully."

"I believe her spirit is here with us, cheering for our little get-together," Soraya replied pensively.

Within the stillness of the night, we could hear the distant sounds of the sea mixing with our shared memories. Each wave seemed to recount a moment with Beatrice: the morning salutations, the holiday and birthday cards, the pep talks when we felt like impostors, and the late-night chats about anything and everything. Good things flowed forth from her like a fountain, like a drop of nectar on a parched tongue. I found solace in knowing that Vincent and Soraya saw the same exemplary person I did.

"One thing that Beatrice left to us was the case report on the thirty-two-year-old with extrapulmonary sarcoidosis.

How're things going with that?" I asked, curious yet careful, wanting to change the subject to something lighter.

Vincent cleared his throat, his gaze falling to the grass below his feet.

"Well, it's definitely still a work in progress. Beatrice was the glue holding it all together. We're missing a puzzle piece without her, but we still need to finish it. It's what she would've wanted."

"Dr. Coffman talked to me about the write-up the other day," Soraya interjected, the corners of her mouth quivering. "He wants to dedicate any publications from this work to Beatrice, considering all the groundwork she did."

"Really? That's amazing," I said, radiating with a hard-to-hide happiness.

"I think I remember that now," Vincent responded. "Maybe our best path forward would be to split up the sections of the paper to divide and conquer."

The idea perked me up, a revived project that could give us a path to channel our mourning into something Beatrice loved.

"That would be great," I said. "I think that'll set us up for success."

As the night wore on, we found ourselves reminiscing about Beatrice, the good times painted in vivid hues, and the realization of her absence in a solid gray. Funny moments from past didactic sessions, desperate deadlines met with Beatrice's unyielding optimism, and evenings spent as a group under these very stars.

"We should gather for these dinners more often," Soraya suggested. "It would be like a tribute to her, keeping the fire burning brightly."

"Beatrice did like her traditions," I replied, feeling a light chuckle escape me as I thought of how she would fuss to make each gathering perfect.

"Then it's settled," Vincent concluded. "This will be our new tradition: making a meal together and enjoying it—for her and us."

Our unconditional positive regard for one another made me feel a slight easing in the part of my soul where grief had taken root. Spending time together in remembrance of those we loved, understanding Vincent and Soraya's struggles, and planning a future tribute to keep Beatrice's spirit alive—all of these things were deeply engraved in our collective journey, and we would solve any problems on our journey together.

As the twilight bled into darkness on the evening before the assault, I awaited news that did not come. The strange, undefined movement to the south that the scouts had reported—a ghostly specter threatening in its ambiguity—gnawed at my thoughts. Despite bolstering the defenses and doubling the watch, a cold dread touched the edges of my heart. The moon hung like a traitor in the sky, prematurely aged to an ominous orange hue that reminded me of the ancient prophecies. These prophecies spoke of an uprising led by a shadow born of royal blood but cast aside: Draconius.

The siege that was born out of the darkness was overwhelming. It commenced with the swiftness of a hawk's descent. The watchtowers, reinforced under my direct command, were no match against the obscured enemy's fire bombs. Death rained from the sky as the castle's sturdy oak gates and stone walls were battered by the relentless archers hiding in the cover of the night. Amid the chaos, I hastened to the courtyard to lead and inspire my army, but fate was cruel. The smoke was potent, the heat unbearable, and the very stones of my castle wept fiery tears. An explosion near the palace's eastern wing sent a barrage of stone flying through the air, one sizable piece plummeting directly toward me.

Here I now lay, my kingdom literally upon me, crushing the breath from my chest. The scent of charred wood and flesh choked the air. The screams of my people and the clash of steel against steel echoed around the once-pristine court, which had now been transmogrified into a sordid butcher's floor. I struggled futilely against the stone, pinning me down as a shadow enveloped me, blocking out the rampant destruction. The figure, ominous and steady with a battle ax gleaming, looked supernatural—a vengeful spirit sent from the depths of Hell to claim me as its war trophy. The added weight pressed the air from my lungs when it climbed upon me, anchoring me irrevocably to my doomed fate.

As the ax glinted, descending like the final verdict of a tyrannous judge, I glimpsed the eerily familiar features of my executioner. A horrifying realization dawned upon me in my final seconds. Those contours echoed my own—it was like staring into a twisted mirror reflecting my own countenance, like my doppelganger. With the last fleeting breath, the prophecy's final stroke fell sharper than the executioner's ax—it was not my kingdom or crown but my heart and soul that were commanded to pay the true price for a crown's folly. The shadow of a buried reality claimed what it was owed.

CHAPTER SEVENTEEN

Fall, with Head Trauma

> *Without the hammer of experience to temper its wild imagination, the fool is disillusioned, broken, and lost in the sound and fury surrounding it.*

Emergency medicine was my second rotation in my third year. During the first week of August, I was scheduled for a graveyard shift with Dr. Gregory Madrid. Switching abruptly from working days to nights had left me torpid at the beginning of the twelve hours I had before me. Sipping on a tart energy drink, I wearily took the chart of an elderly woman who had an unwitnessed fall at home.

She had been transported to the hospital by ambulance when a neighbor went to check on her. As I reviewed the woman's chart, I could see that she had a history of osteoporosis and had previously fractured her hip. I knew that falls for older adults were often a serious matter and could lead to complications. I quickly made my way to her room, where I found the frail and vulnerable woman lying in bed.

"Can you tell me what happened leading up to your fall?" I asked after introducing myself and pulling up a chair next to her bed.

Mrs. Jenkins looked up at me with a pained and disoriented expression.

"I was trying to reach for a jar on the top shelf in the kitchen and lost my balance," she said softly. "I heard a loud crack when I fell, and I couldn't get up by myself."

I nodded empathetically, understanding the fear and helplessness she must have felt.

"Tell me more. What was going on with your loss of balance? Did you feel any dizziness or a rapid heartbeat at any point?"

She lowered her head, trying to cast her mind back to the moments before the fall.

"I recall feeling chest heaviness and some shortness of breath right before," Mrs. Jenkins answered with some hesitancy in her voice. "I've never experienced anything quite like that. Now that I think about it, I also remember feeling pretty scared. But that's all. I can't remember anything else until Mark found me."

"So, you probably aren't sure if you hit your head when you fell, correct?"

"That's right," she said, frowning at her uncertainty. "I have no clue. My right elbow hurts, but I don't have a headache or neck pain if that's helpful."

"That is," I said before performing a focused neurological examination.

Good, I thought. *No deficits.*

"We'll get you some answers and work to rule out what we can," I explained. "We'll start with imaging of your head and elbow, blood work, and an EKG. We will also measure your vital signs while lying down, sitting, and standing."

Mrs. Jenkins agreed with the plan. After making a few notes to myself, I moved back to the workstation Dr. Madrid was still sitting at to run the plan past him. With his recommendations, I got on one of the computers and ordered the tests I had described to Mrs. Jenkins. Since the results would take a while, I spent extra time with Mrs. Jenkins, talking about her life and listening to her stories.

In my follow-up conversation, I realized Mrs. Jenkins had no family nearby to support her; only her neighbors lived close to her. It broke my heart to think of her going through this ordeal alone, and I pictured myself in her shoes in those moments before her fall. She had lived a full and adventurous life, traveling the world and working as a teacher for over thirty years before retiring. Her husband of almost fifty years tragically passed away in a motor vehicle accident when the two of them still lived in Baltimore.

"Doctor, would you mind if I took the patient back for her CT scan and X-ray?" a radiology technology student bashfully asked, sliding open the door to Mrs. Jenkins' room.

"Not at all. That takes priority," I responded, standing and clearing the way for the team to take her back for her imaging. "Mrs. Jenkins, I'll be back when we have your results."

While Mrs. Jenkins was undergoing her diagnostic tests, I grabbed another chart and went to see a young girl with ear pain. After establishing a diagnosis of acute otitis media, I conferred with Dr. Madrid before prescribing an oral antibiotic and discharging the patient so she could get home and sleep. After wrapping up with the next patient, I returned to my computer, keen to see the results of Mrs. Jenkins' workup. Fortunately, there was no sign of intracranial hemorrhaging on her CT scan, no fractures on her elbow X-ray, and no major abnormalities on her panel of blood work. Her orthostatic vital signs were all normal, too. However, her EKG revealed a likely source of the syncope.

"Looking at the left-sided precordial leads," I asserted, showing Dr. Madrid the EKG, "I appreciate left ventricular hypertrophy with a strain pattern. Over here, there is some clearer evidence of left atrial enlargement."

"So, what do you think is going on?" Dr. Madrid quizzed me, a twinkle of pride already in his eyes.

"Symptomatic aortic stenosis," I answered, confident in my words. "Highly suggested, but pending confirmation."

In my mind, I pictured the significant narrowing of the large artery as it exits the heart and how that narrowing prevented blood from flowing as it normally would to the rest of the body, including the brain.

"I agree. We should admit this patient and consult the cardiology team after ordering a transthoracic echocardiogram to look for structural abnormalities, especially at the valves. She may need an urgent aortic valve replacement."

Before we could continue discussing Mrs. Jenkins's situation, the indubitable thud of someone hitting the ground stole our attention.

"Dr. Madrid, we need your help over here!" a man's voice called out from the other side of the emergency department. "Valerie just collapsed!"

Dr. Madrid stared at me as we stopped typing in admission orders at our workstations. Without exchanging a single word, we dashed down the hall and around the nurse's station to find five nurses and an emergency medical technician gathered around Valerie, the charge nurse on duty tonight.

"She fell about ten seconds ago and hit her head on the desk on the way down," Nathan, one of the other nurses, reported in a shaky voice. "I couldn't get to her in time to catch her."

Dr. Madrid quickly knelt beside Valerie, checking her pulse and breathing. I noticed a large contusion on her forehead from where she struck the desk. He then assessed her level of consciousness and looked for any other potential injuries.

"Valerie, can you hear me?" he loudly asked, trying to elicit a reaction.

Valerie's eyes fluttered open, but she seemed disoriented.

"Can you tell me what day it is?" he asked gently.

Valerie shook her head slightly, unable to give a coherent response.

"I-i-it hurts," she stammered, reaching for the base of her skull.

"Let's get her over to the trauma bay," Dr. Madrid instructed the team, pointing to a nearby bed.

As the team moved Valerie, I asked one of the nurses to start an intravenous line and hook her up to a cardiac monitor. Our team worked quickly and efficiently, taking Valerie's vital signs and performing a thorough physical exam. Dr. Madrid remained calm and composed, providing clear instructions and guidance to the team. I noticed something particularly surprising on my physical exam.

"Positive passive nuchal rigidity and Brudzinski sign," I reported to Dr. Madrid, already building out my differential diagnosis as we continued to evaluate her. "I'm worried about a subarachnoid hemorrhage."

"I am, too," Dr. Madrid admitted after repeating the exam maneuvers. "Let's wheel over for a stat CT scan. Nathan, can you call radiology to let them know we're on our way?"

As we marched over to the radiology department while carefully guiding Valerie's bed, we all feared the worst yet hoped for something minor—a fainting spell, exhaustion from overwork, or dehydration. However, the subtleties of her symptoms and findings on examination suggested something more severe, like a brain bleed. She was intermittently responsive, slurring her words with a distant gaze. The anxious buzz in the room was palpable as I helped Dr. Madrid roll Valerie into the CT room.

"Let's look at what we're dealing with," Dr. Madrid muttered, trying to keep his professional poise while his hands trembled slightly.

Dr. Madrid and I went over to the viewing screen as the scanner whirred and clicked, creating images of Valerie's brain.

When the images finally loaded, his chilling, sharp inhale struck a grim chord.

"Oh, no," Dr. Madrid said under his breath, pointing to a horizontal cross-section of her brain.

There it was: a glaring bright white signal indicating bleeding in multiple areas within the brain. That was the subarachnoid hemorrhage.

In moments like these, priorities crystallize with a terrifying clarity.

"I see that, too," I murmured, feeling a cold line of sweat dripping down my back even though the room was chilly. "Thankfully, I don't see any skull fractures or other bleeds from the fall. I bet she had a spontaneous hemorrhage and then collapsed. We need to consult neurosurgery. I'll give them a call."

Our neurosurgery team consisted of a mobile unit based at a key medical center two hours away, another brutal reality of working in a less equipped facility. Dr. Madrid and I stabilized Valerie as we awaited their initial assessments via electronic communication. We administered medications to manage her blood pressure and prevent further bleeding and prepared for the highly likely scenario of transferring her for surgery.

Dr. Caleb Edwards, our neurosurgical consultant on call, confirmed our fears and recommended immediate transfer.

"It looks like you've caught it early enough," his voice crackled through the speakerphone. "She needs surgery to evacuate the blood, but we can't do it. Once she's stabilized, transfer her to the next available medical center with neurosurgical capability."

Processing logistical concerns all while ensuring Valerie's immediate survival presented a circus of multitasking. Given the urgency, we contacted the nearest trauma center with neurosurgical capability and arranged for a helicopter transfer. We kept up the treatment to maintain her stable vital signs. Hours later, we received word that the emergency medical helicopter was about to land at our heliport. All at once, several emergency medical technicians came in to transport Valerie. We walked with the receiving team to the heliport until it was time to transition care completely.

"Thank you, Dr. Madrid and everyone else," Valerie weakly whispered as we prepared to leave her side.

Dr. Madrid smiled warmly at her, his eyes reflecting fulfillment and pride in his work. As the helicopter took off, its lights flickering against the dark, drizzly sky, the stress of the situation slowly dissipated, leaving everyone involved tired and relieved. Dr. Madrid placed a reassuring hand on my shoulder.

"We did everything we could at this point," he declared. "Now it's up to the next team to continue management. What a night, am I right?"

Left behind were the anxiety and adrenaline, and a waiting game began. The hospital staff started a prayer chain, which was full of both hope and dread. But the show had to go on, so I cracked my knuckles before diving back into caring for patients. After seeing five more patients in the emergency department after Valerie, I became exhausted, not having adjusted to working this late.

"I'm going to use the restroom," I said as Dr. Madrid gave me a thumbs-up to show he heard me.

With stiff muscles, I rose from my chair and strolled across the unit to the nearest staff restroom. After locking the door, I walked over to the sink to splash water on my face. My eyes were bloodshot from looking at a computer screen for so long. Being in this emergency department still caused me discomfort after what happened to Beatrice just over a month ago. I looked at myself and my ragged appearance as wisps of memories crept back into my conscious mind. From somewhere else in the unit, I could hear the high-pitched screech of a cardiac monitor.

The shrill sound transported me back to the moment I watched the resuscitation attempt and the conversation I had with Alexandra Quintana right afterward. The steadily increasing palpitations caused pressure to build up in my chest. My breaths became shallower and more rapid as my thoughts raced across my mind as if speeding along the Autobahn in Germany. I gripped my chest as my vision became blurry. The next thing I knew, I was falling backward before everything went dark.

"You're coming around," Nathan spoke excitedly, touching my shoulder. "You scared us."

"What happened?" I questioned, discombobulated from recent events. "My head is killing me."

As if perceiving a change in my condition from halfway across the unit, Dr. Madrid entered the room with a worried look.

"Thank goodness! You're finally awake! How're you feeling?" Dr. Madrid asked, clearly relieved.

"In some pain," I disclosed, reaching for the back of my head only to touch some gauze. "Did I hit my head when I lost consciousness?"

"You did," Dr. Madrid nodded. "We're not exactly sure what happened since we found you down and unconscious. That was about twenty-five minutes ago. I'm pretty sure you syncopized."

"I think it was a severe panic attack," I stated, placing my hand over my chest to jog my memory. "I had palpitations, chest pressure, hyperventilation, blurry vision, and then loss of consciousness."

"Do you know what triggered it?"

"The alarm of the cardiac monitor when there's an abnormality," I confessed. "It took me back to when Beatrice died."

After a series of tests and monitoring, Dr. Madrid had ruled out other potential causes of my loss of consciousness, concluding that a severe panic attack was the most likely etiology. As I lay in the hospital bed, surrounded by beeping monitors and white walls, I reflected on how I had reached this point. I realized I had been neglecting my own needs in favor of taking care of everyone else and had been avoiding my demons as a result. Apart from my sessions with Dr. Price, I had put my mental and emotional well-being on the back burner. But now, faced with the reality of my mortality, I knew things had to change. I needed to prioritize my health and happiness, no matter how busy or stressful life happened to be. I needed to honor what I said to Dr. Altamura.

WHILE SITTING IN BED AS DR. MADRID EXPERTLY STAPLED the wound on the back of my scalp, I vowed to reclaim my inner peace. To do this, I planned to spend the weekend focusing on a solitary writing retreat and forest bathing. This decision led me into the reposeful embraces of Elderson Forest, a place often visited by locals and tourists for its watercolor painting-like qualities and seclusion.

As I entered its green labyrinth, the towering pines and the chirping cicadas welcomed me with open arms. I had reserved a small cabin near a river known for its enchanted tranquility. This forest would be my writer's retreat: the balm for my frayed heart and scattered mind. Upon my arrival, the river's harmonious babble struck me. It was as if the water spoke in angelic whispers that my soul needed to hear. After making it inside the cabin, I unpacked my belongings: a notebook, several pens, and my laptop, which had a blank Word document loaded up.

In the unseasonable coolness of the forest, I walked along the riverside, absorbing the essence of the place. I could feel the soft crunch of leaves and twigs underfoot, see the ripple of the water over rocks, and hear the playful calls of birds. Nature was alive and spectacularly indifferent to the artificial urgencies of human life. Choosing a stop beside an ancient oak, I sat cross-legged on the forest floor and opened my notebook.

What do you feel? I prompted myself.

My pen hovered over the blank page, then danced: I wrote about the zesty scent of pine, about the whisper of the river that spoke of continuance and mindfulness, and about the nuanced movements of the summer leaves. Each word disconnected me from my recent turmoil and rethreaded me into the fabric of the present. My breath synchronized with the rhythmic flow of the river. My thoughts cleared, mimicking the cloudless sky above. For the first time in months, my heart did not feel like a clenched fist, beating like the hooves of a racehorse in my chest.

As the sun began to dip, casting longer shadows and painting the sky in gradients of orange and indigo, I packed up and headed back to the cabin. The evening of desired solitude was contemplative, filled with an unspoken promise to return to my writing the next morning. Both afternoons I was there, I reviewed and typed out my day's handwritten revelations, turning visceral experiences into structured stories on paper. That weekend, I wrote ardently, not about imagined adventures or fictional catastrophes but about real sensations and emotions. My words were their own entities, as though they carried the essence of the forest within them, healing me with every letter typed and every page filled.

A sense of profound accomplishment enveloped me as I wrapped up my final musings and packed away my laptop. The panic that had once constricted my chest had loosened into something much more manageable. My hands, usually steady only during medical procedures, had found a new life: bringing my experiences to life on paper. I had dissected my fears, isolated my joys, and prescribed myself the most effective medicine of all—self-expression. As I locked the door to the little cabin one final time, I knew Elderson Forest had inscribed a permanent, vivacious script in my life's story, reminding me that sometimes the best way to address the chaos of life is to retreat, reflect, and write it all down.

Early Monday morning, the gentle hum of the hospital came to life, with nurses starting their shifts and patients beginning to stir. I returned to the inpatient teaching service after my brief weekend respite. As Alta Vista Hospital roared to life with the prospects of a new day, I aligned myself back into the rhythm of my clinical duties. When I pulled up the patient list on the digital dashboard, my heart skipped as "Vivian Jenkins" blinked softly against the backlit screen.

It had been several days since I had admitted her, and my mind raced with concern over her condition. On admitting her, surrounded by the sterile white of the emergency department and under the harsh glare of overhead lights, I wanted to make sure to follow up with her, even if I was not the one to provide her care directly. Entering her room on the fourth floor, I was relieved as sunlight poured through the open window, casting warm rays across the bed where Mrs. Jenkins sat upright, reading a magazine.

"Good morning, Mrs. Jenkins," I greeted her, my voice a mixture of professional warmth and genuine care. "How are you today?"

"Having a good time reading all of these celebrity stories as if I didn't have a care in the world," she chuckled, setting her magazine aside. "It's so nice to see you again. I was sure I wouldn't after they got me over here."

"I see you've been keeping yourself entertained," I smiled, taking a seat at her bedside. "What ended up happening after you were admitted?"

"Well, you all were right about that aortic valve," Mrs. Jenkins responded, beaming at me. "It was severely narrow on the echo, and the cardiologist told me how bad things could've gone had we waited even one more day. The interventional cardiologist got involved in my care and performed what I think is called a 'TAVR.' Since then, I have been feeling much better. My hospital doctor says I should be able to get out of here sometime today."

"That's fantastic," I said, leaning back in the chair. "I'm so glad you're doing so much better. That's what matters above all else."

She shook her head slowly, a wide grin parting her lips.

"You're a special kind of doctor," she told me, staring straight into my eyes. "You didn't have to do any of this. I'm sure you're really busy today, and your taking the time to see me means more than you can imagine. Today, you treated me like a person instead of a meat bag with problems that need to be solved. Thank you so much for that."

As I walked from her room, her thanks echoed in my brain. It reminded me why I had chosen this path—to make a difference, heal, and connect. Each patient's story was a thread in the tapestry of my career, but some threads—like the one with Mrs. Jenkins—were woven with brilliant hues that shimmered with a pronounced brightness. Even though our healthcare system was set up for winners and losers depending on the size of the bank account, interactions like these sustained me.

Several weeks after Mrs. Jenkins was discharged from the hospital, I learned that Valerie returned to work, her smile weaker but undefeated. Her recovery was slow but progressive, a testament not just to the skilled hands that operated on her but to the swift actions taken by her friends and colleagues at our modest Alta Vista Hospital. In medicine, a moment's decision can save a life: a sobering truth now solidified in each of our hearts.

CHAPTER EIGHTEEN

Reflections

> *Only when it avails itself to someone who can provide the opportunity for this essential growth does it find the capacity to flourish, which causes all resistance to appear as navigable waves on a sea filled with incomprehensible mysteries of which we only hope to fathom pieces.*

I sat absorbed in my task on a lazy Saturday morning at the Frieden Bay Library. The library was an oasis along the bay, with daylight filtering gently through the vaulted glass and casting playful shadows across the wooden floors. I was typing out the final draft of the research study—a project close to my heart—that Beatrice had initiated many months ago after our disappointing meeting with the Alta Vista CEO. Beatrice, Dr.

Mose, Dr. Calisto, and I had conceptualized this project over a year ago when Beatrice and I were early in our second year of training, still somewhat fresh-faced and eager to make a difference in the world of healthcare.

With her deep interest in applying public health frameworks to primary care, Beatrice had always been passionate about the social determinants of health—a body of work examining how socioeconomic conditions, education, neighborhood and physical environments, employment, and social support networks affect health. Her intensity and concern for these often-overlooked aspects inspired us all to act, and this paper culminated that effort.

In this study, we aimed to implement a standardized questionnaire at the Primary Care Center to evaluate each patient's social needs that might impact their health, ranging from financial instability to inadequate housing. Based on the responses, we connected our patients with a social worker we had hired specifically for this role. This integration was a novel approach in our local healthcare system and the public health and medical literature more broadly. In addition to preparing this manuscript in hopes of getting it published in an academic journal, I submitted an abstract for consideration as an oral presentation at a national conference in our specialty.

As I scrolled through the manuscript document, my eyes fell upon the sections that Beatrice had written. Her words were poignant, reflecting a profound understanding of our patients' hardships. Besides possessing the precision of a well-seasoned researcher, each sentence resonated with her dedication to her work. It was hard to grasp that she was no longer here to see the fruition of her work. I remembered the late nights spent planning the study, the countless revisions of the questionnaire, and the meetings that stretched into hours as we debated the best ways to implement the program. Beatrice had always been there, pushing us forward, her mind a constant storm of ideas and improvements.

As I continued to type, I reflected on my responsibility to honor her memory by ensuring the study's successful publication and, if possible, presentation. Other researchers and clinicians needed to know about this work. This was not just some banal research project; this was Beatrice's legacy. I carefully edited the text, integrating the data we had collected over the previous months. The preliminary results were promising: reductions in hospital readmissions, ameliorated biochemical markers of disease, improved patient satisfaction, and qualitative feedback from the community about positive interactions with the social worker. The final data reinforced these observations, leading to stronger conclusions about the significance of this work.

The library was nearly empty; the usual weekend patrons had chosen to enjoy the day outdoors. Only the soft tapping of my laptop keys and the distant hum of a lawn mower far away disrupted the silence. Lost in thought, I hardly noticed Dr. Mose's approach until she sat across from me.

"Making good progress?" she asked, motioning toward my screen.

I nodded, pushing back the sudden surge of emotions.

"It's going well. Just going through Beatrice's sections. She was a progressive thinker."

Dr. Mose smiled sadly, her eyes reflecting a mutually understood sorrow.

"Yes, she was. This was her passion project, for sure. Speaking of which, how are you holding up?"

"It's tough," I admitted. "Some days are easier; others are harder. Every bit of this reminds me of Beatrice. But, much like Soraya said to Vincent and me a while back, it feels like she's still here, guiding us."

"We owe it to her to finish strong," she said firmly. "Beatrice may not be here physically, but her impact is unquestionably all over this study. It's going to change lives, just like she wanted."

With renewed resolve, I turned back to my manuscript. The rest of the morning passed in a blur of graphs, citations, and discussion points. The study was more than just a one-off in a community-based clinic; it was a message of hope and a strategy for change. Finally, as the draft neared completion, I leaned back in my chair, allowing myself a moment of reflection. Beatrice had left us too soon, but her vision was alive, ready to be communicated to the world. In the stillness of the library, surrounded by Beatrice's words and dreams, I felt a bittersweet blend of loss and purpose. We would publish this study, disseminate the findings, and continue the work she had started. The project would go on, a lasting tribute to a remarkable woman whose legacy would continue to inspire and bring about meaningful change.

As I trod through the dense underbrush of a menacing forest, the sunlight barely pierced through the thick canopy above. Legends had long spoken of the Guardian Tree, an ancient arboreal giant said to house the spirits of the forest. Skeptics dismissed these tales as folklore until a freak storm uncovered its vast trunk one summer. Beatrice and Dr. Altamura had ventured into these woods to study the Guardian Tree. However, their typical check-in call had turned into a static-filled plea for help—their voices echoing strangely from high above the forest floor.

I approached a tree the size of the Willis Tower in Chicago and craned my neck just to see the first branches sprawling like the arms of a colossus into the sky. I could faintly hear Beatrice and Dr. Altamura shouting out from branches much higher up.

"Help us! We're up here!"

The sound was faint, their figures barely visible from such an immense height. The tree's trunk was mammoth, and its bark was smooth—impossible to scale or grip. I circled the tree in frustration, looking for any climbable spot or hidden crevice. Regrettably, sliding down one of its large exposed roots, I ended up with a scratched arm and bruised pride. Just then, a stranger approached me. His attire was odd considering the backdrop: a sleek red tuck-tail tuxedo, almost glowing amid the earthy tones of the forest. He had slicked-back chestnut hair and a mischievous twinkle in his eye.

"Seems like you could use a hand, or perhaps several," he said in a smooth, almost melodious voice.

He offered me a coiled rope, but it was too short. Next came a pair of spiked boots that failed to penetrate the tough bark. Each attempt left me more crestfallen than the last. The stranger watched with piqued curiosity before finally stepping forward with a final offer.

"There is one last thing I can provide," he said, his tone now serious. "But it comes with a painful transformation."

Desperation painted every choice.

"Do it," I urged, unsure what I was agreeing to. "I can take it."

With a nod, he touched my shoulder, and pain seared through my body—an intense, burning agony like no other. I gritted my teeth as bony structures ripped through the skin on my back, unfurling into large, majestic wings feathered in hues of ivory and silver. Testing these new appendages felt alien, yet somehow natural. As I flapped clumsily at first, I began ascending toward the voices of my friends. But my energy drained rapidly, the unfamiliar muscles burning with each beat.

"Just a little more," I gasped, struggling to reach them.

Moments before I could touch their outstretched hands, darkness crept into the edges of my vision, and I plummeted downward. The ground hurtled toward me, and then darkness. When I regained consciousness, I was lying on the ground, back in my normal form. The massive wings were gone, and there was no sign of the mysterious stranger in the red tuxedo.

The Sunday air was crisp, carrying a certain vernal freshness as Soraya, Vincent, and I met outside my small apartment. We had agreed to drive together, wanting to accompany each other on the solemn journey to Beatrice's gravesite about two and a half hours north of Frieden Bay. It had been nearly a year since her passing, and though time had healed the sharpness of our grief, the scar it left was still tender. As we settled into Vincent's aging sport utility vehicle, Soraya turned to us with a light smile.

"I think Bea would've liked today. Do you remember how she loved the spring? She would say it made her feel alive."

Without a word, Vincent nodded and started the engine.

The drive took us through winding roads lined with trees proudly blooming with beautiful spring flowers. As the town's landmarks faded into a blur of countryside, each mile moved us equal parts forward and inward, recalling fragments of Beatrice's vibrant life. She had simultaneously been a force of nature and undeniably herself. When we arrived at the cemetery, the grounds were silent, save for the soft rustling of leaves and the occasional chirp of a distant bird. We walked together, shoulder to shoulder, until we found the graceful headstone that signified Beatrice's resting place. It stood solitary amidst the other graves, differentiated only by its artfully engraved face of polished white marble. The elegance of the monument stood out in my memory from the interment.

I reached out, touching the cold marble, feeling its smoothness against my fingertips. We stood there for a long while, each lost in our memories, until the air grew colder with the approach of a thunderstorm, urging us back to the warmth of the car. It was Vincent who finally broke the silence.

"She'd hate us standing here and being all somber," he said. "Remember Halloween when she convinced us to go as characters from her favorite novel?"

How could we forget? Beatrice's plan for us to attend a costume party in Frieden Bay turned into an unexpected adventure when Beatrice's enthusiasm led us astray into a haunted house, her laughter echoing louder than the spooky sounds around us. The memory brightened our faces, a harmonious warmth filling the cooling air around us with our stories and love. As we drove back, conversations flowed about the old times—the pranks, the late-night movie marathons, and Beatrice's endless quirks and charms. A realization settled gently among us, much like the dusk softening the edges of the day; though Beatrice was gone, the essence of her spirit continued to thread through our lives, as meaningful as ever.

After visiting Beatrice's grave, the air around me still lingered with the mournful echo of goodbye. Beatrice had been not just a colleague but a steadfast friend and visionary in our field. The somber trip to the cemetery helped me feel connected to her, to remind me that the void her passing left was both personal and professional. Back in my apartment, I settled into my well-worn chair, the soft whir of my laptop accompanying my return to the mundane. I had emails to check—a task perennially lying in wait. With a steaming cup of green tea flavored with lemon juice, I attempted to ground myself in the normalcy of the task.

The rich aroma of the tea blunted the rough edges of my melancholy. As I scrolled through various subject lines, one notably stood out—instantly knotting my stomach with a mixture of nervous anticipation and excitement. It was the decision letter from the review committee of the renowned national conference to which I submitted an abstract on the social determinants of health project for an oral presentation. Several long moments passed as I sat staring at the unopened email. With a shaky breath, I clicked open the email.

My eyes quickly scanned the content, searching for a key phrase that would seal the fate of our work. There it was: "We are pleased to inform you…" A surge of relief flowed through me, combined with a pang of sorrow that Beatrice was not here to share this moment. Reinvigorated with purpose, I contacted Dr. Mose and Dr. Calisto. After congratulating me on the decision, Dr. Mose promised to help in any way she could from afar due to prior commitments. Dr. Calisto, equally enthusiastic about our cause and always a voice of reason, agreed to join me in Washington, D.C., to co-present our work.

"This is incredible," Dr. Calisto praised me, pride imbuing each word. "I would love to join you for this. It would be a way to get closure with everything related to the program, and what's better is that I can do that with you."

THE DRIVE TO THE CONFERENCE WITH DR. CALISTO WAS a reflective one. We reminisced about Beatrice's unparalleled commitment to what originally started as a simple quality improvement project and thought about how she would have been overjoyed by the advocacy our project was bringing to the challenges faced by patients living with barriers created by their social conditions. Upon arrival, the conference buzzed with the energy of knowledge exchange and professional networking. We spent the first day participating in workshops and talks on building research capacity in community-based family medicine residency programs, using individualized learning plans to normalize academic goal-setting, and protecting psychological safety in the clinical learning environment.

After a busy day of learning, Dr. Calisto and I had dinner at a bistro on our hotel's first floor. After agonizing over the extensive menu details, Dr. Calisto and I looked at each other. We fell on the same combination of à la carte items: French onion soup with a mushroom, cheese, and chicken panini. He and I laughed as we reflected on our journeys through undergraduate medical education. At one point, Dr. Calisto shamefully admitted to unhinged benders that resulted in hangovers during major tests. I always appreciated Dr. Calisto's ability to relate to others, whether they were peers, learners, or friends. As we finished our sandwich and soup, our conversation changed to our impending presentation.

"How are you feeling about tomorrow? Nervous?" he inquired, his support for me clear in his expression. "I'm here to support you in any way possible, even if that means sitting on the bench and letting the star run the show."

"I'm feeling okay," I said, not being honest.

I felt Dr. Calisto's incredulous stare upon me, which made my shoulder tense up.

"But, a part of me is worried about not doing a good job and dishonoring Beatrice," I added more truthfully.

"There's no way you'll dishonor her," he challenged me. "The fact that you and I are here in our nation's capital for this conference proves that you have already done everything you need to show her respect."

"You're right," I conceded, my body relaxing from Dr. Calisto's encouragement. "I should focus on what we've already accomplished and not keep my eyes always fixed on the next goalpost."

With that, we decided I would present most of the slides, and then Dr. Calisto would come in to deliver his summary remarks and answer the audience's questions. As my head hit my pillow that night, I fell asleep quickly, ready to knock the presentation out of the park in the morning.

When our moment to present arrived, Dr. Calisto and I stood before our peers, a presentation clicker in my unsteady hand serving as a testament to the bittersweet tinge of our achievements. I started the presentation with a note of dedication.

"We stand here today, proud to present a vision significantly shaped by an incredible researcher and a dear friend, Dr. Beatrice Portinari, whose work aimed to bridge the gap in health disparities influenced by social determinants," I said authoritatively. "Though she is no longer with us, her spirit lives on through this project."

Attentive silence gripped the room, our words about real change resonating with many in attendance. I continued, detailing the methodology and potential impact of our findings. The session ended with eloquent summary statements from Dr. Calisto and a robust discussion, which underscored that there was crucial work to be done and that we were merely at the threshold. The conference was a professional success and a personal tribute: a celebration of a journey once walked by two friends, which is now continued in honor of one. I realized

Beatrice's legacy was not encapsulated solely within the gravestone that bore her name, but in every stride we took forward from the groundwork she laid. Following our presentation, Dr. Calisto and I headed to a café near the convention center for lunch. His effervescent behavior gave me insight into how well he thought we did.

"That went very well," he remarked, stuffing his mouth with a croque monsieur. "I think we may be a strong contender for the award in the 'Population & Community Health' category."

"I really hope we win," I said, sipping my glass of iced tea. "But even if we don't, just being here is victory enough."

We clinked our drinking glasses together and then focused on our repast. Dr. Calisto's phone vibrated vigorously on the hardwood table, drawing our attention away from the food scraps on our plates. He snatched up his phone to read the message he had received. Without words, he turned his phone screen around to show me the message.

"Hot off the press," he uttered, remaining stoic.

I looked closely at his screen and made out the most important word: *Award*.

"I can't believe it!" I exclaimed, nearly vaulting over the table to embrace the man who had been my Program Director. "We did it! Aren't those certificates presented on the main stage?"

"Yes," he answered, an exultant grin breaking upon his face. "We should head back to the hotel to freshen up before the ceremony this evening. I'll meet you in the lobby around 6:00, okay?"

My heart soared as we returned to the hotel. This was a major achievement independent of the more personal motivations behind it. Dr. Calisto and I triumphantly walked back to the convention center and made our way to the main stage, where the award recipients had reserved seats right at the front. After a few prefatory comments from the president of our professional society, we walked over to the stage to accept the framed certificates. Our steps seemed to echo as we set foot on the stage to receive our award for "Best Research Project in Population & Community Health." The spotlight felt intensely bright, blurring the faces in the crowd into a sea of indistinct colors and shapes. My heart raced—not from the accolades nor the audience, but from knowing we were achieving something that would have made Beatrice proud.

Aware of the sentimental value of this moment, Dr. Calisto placed a supportive hand on my back as we accepted the award.

"You're making a remarkable difference, just as she always knew you would," he whispered loud enough for me to hear.

Those words—simple yet profound—filled me with a poignant mix of joy and sorrow.

Later that evening, after the crowd had dispersed and the echoes of congratulations had faded, Dr. Calisto and I shared a quiet celebratory dinner at a small restaurant overlooking the Potomac River. It was a perfect place for reflection—both personal and across the shimmering waters before us.

"You know, there's so much I never got a chance to tell you as Program Director that I should have," Dr. Calisto said, his dark eyes twinkling in the soft light. "I've seen many residents come and go during my tenure, but your dedication is exceptional. Your commitment to your patients and colleagues is unlike anything I have seen. When you finish your training at the end of June, our profession will gain a major asset with you. I know you'll contribute to our specialty in an outsized way."

"Thank you, Dr. Calisto," I replied, deeply moved by Dr. Calisto's heartfelt praise. "Although, I have always found it ironic that you call some of your residents 'once-in-a-lifetime talents' or predict 'outsized' contributions from them in the future when *you* are one of the greats."

Once dinner concluded, we continued our conversation while strolling along the Potomac River. The evening was cool, the sky just beginning to sprinkle stars across its dark canvas. We stopped at the riverside, watching the water flow endlessly onward. In the gentle lapping of the waves against the shore, I saw it there—a reflection in the river that took my breath away. Beatrice's face appeared on the water's surface for a fleeting moment, her smile as radiant as I remembered. I teared up from seeing her again, even in this incorporeal form.

In my mind, I could hear my conversation with Beatrice's mother during the wake.

"She loved being a doctor, didn't she?" Isabella had asked quietly, searching my eyes for confirmation.

"Yes, more than anything," I had replied. *"She made a difference and touched so many lives."*

Isabella had nodded, wiping away a few tears.

"That's all she ever wanted."

"That," I had affirmed, *"she certainly achieved."*

Dr. Calisto noticed my silence and followed my gaze to the water. He did not see what I saw, but he understood.

"She's always with you in everything you do. And she always will be."

"Always," I repeated quietly, watching as the visage blended into the water.

CHAPTER NINETEEN

Broken Vessels

In the days after the conference, my thoughts of Beatrice continued. Though I knew she would be proud of what we had accomplished, a deep pain still ate away at me. As I returned home, my thoughts took a turn toward the depressing, and my body and mind became dysfunctional husks. Unable to sleep again, I got out of bed before the crack of dawn on Sunday and sat motionless on my couch, staring deeply into my mug of black tea. Every passing day since Beatrice's death left me feeling emptier. Momentous occasions like the conference refilled this vessel, allowing it to serve its function. However, the water would inevitably leak out through its many cracks, leaving it empty once again.

My energy was gone. My sleep had become completely disturbed. I could barely eat. I felt like a failure for letting her die. Like I had betrayed the friendship I had with her.

I turned down the opportunity to take another bike ride with Vincent and Soraya; I just could not muster the energy to do it. The thought of going to the clinic tomorrow made me feel even worse; my patients could not see me like this. The haunting memories of Beatrice's unconscious body lying on the pavement next to her car still plagued my mind. The glass pipe. The crumpled aluminum foil. The piercing blue color of the fentanyl. These images indelibly carved into my brain.

As I continued to sit in the oppressive silence, sipping my tea and lost in my thoughts, I could not shake the guilt and regret that consumed me. Beatrice was an outstanding physician and person, destined for greatness in family medicine and happiness in her career. I had tried to help her; I really had. But it was not good enough: I should have noticed the signs of her substance use disorder before the fatal event occurred. It had slipped through my fingers, and now she was gone. Being a physician meant that I could save lives, but in the case of Beatrice, I had failed in almost every regard. I could not save her.

I glanced at the clock and saw that it was almost 6:00 am. The sky was beginning to lighten outside, casting a soft glow through my living room windows. I knew that I could not go on like this, wallowing in my grief and self-pity. I had to get up and move around, find something to occupy my thoughts. Eventually, healing would happen—just not at this moment.

Migrating to my kitchen to get some fresh fruit, I was overcome with grief as my mind wandered to Dr. Altamura.

Although his death from a pulmonary embolism was an unfortunate complication of his orthopedic surgeries and immobilization, losing a beloved mentor and phenomenal family physician left an irreconcilable hollowness deep within my core. He was a veritable force in our specialty. Even though he had died, I continued to emulate his example with everything I did in my care of our community's patients. Dr. Altamura profoundly impacted me as my mentor, guiding me through the ins and outs of family medicine and instilling a deep sense of empathy and compassion for those in need. His dedication to his patients was unmatched, and his knowledge and skill as a physician were second to none.

As I stood in my kitchen, holding a ripe Fuji apple in my hand, heart-warming memories of Dr. Altamura flooded my mind. I remembered the countless hours we spent together in the clinic, seeing patient after patient and sharing their joys and sorrows. I remembered how he always took the time to listen to his patients, going above and beyond to ensure that everyone who walked through his doors received the best possible care. Most of all, I remembered how he inspired me to be a better physician—to strive for excellence in everything I did and to never lose sight of the importance of compassion and empathy in medicine. Dr. Altamura was more than just a mentor to me; he was a friend, a confidant, and a guiding light on my journey.

As I took a bite of the apple, the sweetness of the fruit mingling with the bitterness of my grief, I made a silent vow to carry on the legacies of my beloved friends. I would continue caring for our patients with the same dedication and compassion they had shown them. I would continue to strive for excellence in my practice, always putting the needs of my patients first. I discarded the leftover apple core before returning to the couch, where I felt a sudden fatigue overtake me.

I grabbed the multicolored knitted blanket lying over the back of the couch, covered myself with it, and lowered myself onto the decorative throw pillows. My eyes lost focus as they fixed on the texture of the ceiling. I stared for so long that my corneas and sclerae became dry and irritated, and before me, the whirling of the room in a vertiginous pattern made my abdomen tense with deeply distressing nausea. I shut my eyes quickly to alleviate the effects of the spinning. When I opened them again, I looked through smudged glass onto a barren field where a single individual marched across it.

THE FLASHLIGHT'S POWER WANED AS HE CONTINUED through the desolate wasteland, searching for any shelter he could use for the night. His fallen comrades lay strewn across the ravaged theater of war in the aftermath of the massacre. Miraculously, he was unharmed: no embedded shrapnel, lacerations, or fractures from blunt forces. He had to survive this and avenge his fallen brethren. First, he just needed to find out what had done this to them, what had laid waste to everything he loved.

A miasma of blood and gunpowder permeated the air, making it difficult to breathe. Never had he seen such a catastrophic scene, one that was permanently etching itself into his memory. As he approached a large stone tower and quickly ascended the ladder, the sight of corpses scattered across the soil filled him with intense nausea, each representing the life of someone important to many survivors. Upon reaching the top of the tower, he weakly pulled himself into the small room that served as the sniper's nest. The deceased watchman lay contorted in one corner, apparently the victim of a severe traumatic blow. He averted his gaze, unwilling to let that horrific image further scar his already traumatized psyche.

He picked up a heavily damaged bolt-action rifle from the floor and peered through the scope. He examined the ruins of his company's camp with a few slight adjustments to the scope and scanned the murky environment for any movement. *Where had that damned beast gone? Where had that beast that had taken all these innocent lives gone?* It was as if Satan himself had placed that monster on Earth to wreak havoc upon all it encountered.

He froze as he swept his sight across the perimeter and detected nothing. *It could not have vanished.* In a few seconds, something amorphous caught his attention. He squinted to better look at a dark blob moving in the distance. *That must be it. What else could it be?* The blob stalled briefly, giving him enough time to line it up between the black crosshairs. He breathed a single breath. This was the end for this unholy beast. He snapped his finger across the steel trigger and looked on as the bullet penetrated the blob. The blob wailed in agony and collapsed to the dirt.

"Finally, it's over," he whispered, sighing with deep relief. "The nightmare will soon be over. I just need to see it slain before me."

Scurrying down the tower, he started the grueling trek to the beast's body. Before leaving, he had strapped the rifle to his back and collected a combat knife from a sheath on the watchman, which he now gripped in his hand with a ferocious intensity. *He was a survivor. He was a savior.* It took a long time, but the creature's faint outline eventually appeared over the hill's crest. In anticipation of needing to deliver a killing blow, he readied the knife against his palm and carefully and lightly stepped forward, minimizing the noise produced by his rubber soles crushing the dirt beneath his feet. As he could make out more of the details of the monster, he noted that it was much smaller than expected.

Within a minute, he was upon it. He knelt down and, with a trembling hand, pushed the body over to gaze upon its face.

"NO!" he screamed, left aghast by what he saw. "This can't be real. It can't be you."

"W-w-why?" Dr. Altamura feebly said, grasping at a hemorrhaging wound in his neck.

He could not respond. He was so distraught that he could barely breathe. His mentor's eyes rolled back in his head, and he knew the horrible truth: his mentor was dead, and he had killed him.

He desperately climbed back up to his feet, nearly falling backward as he did so. His hand touched something warm as he frantically tried to regain his footing. Coarse fur rubbed against the skin of his palm, sending a deep chill down his entire body into the pit of his stomach. He froze as he registered the sensations he was experiencing, realizing that he was not alone with Dr. Altamura's body. He felt his heart flutter in his chest as it ramped up its beating. The recent events distorted time and sapped every last drop of his sanity. He half-convinced himself at that moment that he could avoid his imminent demise if he just stood there without moving.

Despite his dubious hope that he had control of this situation, the bear floored him with a single, muscle-packed blow, disarming him in the process. He locked eyes with the ferocious beast as he slammed against the hard-packed earth. He could feel a primal fear sweep through his body. The bear towered above its prey and roared at him with such volume that it temporarily deafened him. As the bear lunged at him, he narrowly dodged the beast and realized that, as he more closely examined it, it bore a false face resembling that of Beatrice.

He reached for the knife as his last resort. The bear returned to its four feet and bellowed once more. Rushing at it, he drove the knife into the bear's flesh, but this did nothing but enrage it. He was at an impasse—this was the bitter end.

He threw his arms up over his face and screamed deafeningly...

I WOKE UP IN A PANIC: A COLD SWEAT CASCADING DOWN my body and my heart pounding. The nightmare I had just experienced felt all too real, like I was living out the final moments of the man in my awful dream. In a daze, I stumbled out of bed and went to the bathroom, my mind racing with confusion and fear. As I stood in front of the mirror, I could barely focus my eyes on my reflection. My face looked pale and drawn—a parallel to the terror I felt inside. I tried to shake off the residual feelings from the nightmare, but they clung to me like a heavy anchor, dragging me down.

Suddenly, the memories from a previous nightmare flooded back to me, vivid and intense. I could see myself knocking on her door, anticipation and dread building in my gut. The door was left slightly ajar, opening further as I made contact with it. I hesitated, not sure what I would find on the other side, but something compelled me to step in. The scene unfolded before my eyes like a twisted movie playing out in my mind. I saw myself walking through her apartment, the air heavy with tension and unease. Shadows flickered on the walls, casting a sense of foreboding over everything. After being transported outside, I saw her lying there, still and silent: a look of peace on her face that belied the tragedy that had befallen her.

I watched as the events from the dream played out in my head, each detail seared into my memory with frightening clarity. The car, the naloxone, the crowd of onlookers, the paramedics rushing to the scene. And then, the flashing lights of the emergency department, the sound of machines beeping in a frantic rhythm, the chaos of the resuscitation bay. And there she was: Beatrice. Now gone right before my eyes. The shock and disbelief hit me in waves, threatening to drown me in a sea of sorrow and regret. I reached out a shaky hand to touch her, to wake her from this nightmare, but she remained still and cold beneath my fingertips.

A rush of guilt crashed into me, accompanied by a deep feeling of loss.

Had I done enough to help her?
Could I have saved her if only I had acted sooner?

The questions swirled around like a relentless storm of doubt and despair. I stumbled back from the mirror, my breath coming in short, ragged gasps. The nightmare pressed down on my shoulders like a boulder, a burden I could not shake. I had to confront the truth of what had happened to find a way to move forward from the nightmares that were consuming me like famished buzzards picking apart carrion in a desert. As I stood there, alone in the darkness of my room, I could not shake the feeling that the nightmare was far from over. The shadows whispered to me, a chilling reminder of the darkness that lurked within me.

You don't deserve happiness. Suffer. Suffer like she did.

And as I closed my eyes, I knew that the nightmare might never truly end.

You'll never escape. No matter how hard you try.

I had to get away to clear my head. Crossing the town in the midday drizzle, I headed toward a trail that tracked along the western cliffside of Frieden Bay. My co-residents and I had hiked across it many times before. As I approached the trail, I parked the car and hurried out in my raincoat as the light rain continued to fall. I hiked for about two miles before reaching the North Wing Promontory. Once there, I slowly shuffled to the promontory's edge and sat down to look over the sea. I sat in absolute silence for several hours, hypnotized by the coordinated movement of the waves striking the rocks beneath me. As I stood up to leave my perch, I heard heavy footsteps behind me.

"Wallowing in your pity, I see," someone said in a voice identical to mine. "You are pathetic and weak."

In the dwindling light of the late afternoon, I turned around to see a shadowy figure leering at me. My heart nearly stopped as I tried to make sense of what I was seeing.

How could someone who sounded and looked like me be standing in front of me?

This anomalous thing could not be real.

"What do you want?" I asked, my voice trembling with fear and confusion.

"Isn't it obvious?" the doppelganger replied, pacing back and forth. "I am here to show you the truth about yourself. You can't escape from who you are and what you have done."

I felt a chill course down my spine. I had come to the trail to clear my head—to escape from the turmoil in my mind—but it seemed that my demons had fled from their cold prisons and followed me here.

"You can't hide from yourself," the doppelganger continued. "You need to face your fears, insecurities, and doubts. Running away will only make them worse."

A potent wave of anger washed over me. I could not stand the sight of this otherworldly being, the sound of its voice that echoed my own.

"Get out of here," I shouted, my fists clenched in defiance. "I don't need your judgment and condescension. Leave me alone!"

The shadowy figure moved toward me, laughing with a cold, mocking sound that made my blood boil.

"You are the fool who thought himself too clever to suffer the natural consequences of this world. You cannot get rid of me so easily; I am a part of you. I'm the embodiment of your darkest and most toxic thoughts. You can't escape from yourself, no matter how hard you try."

I stumbled back, feeling overwhelmed by the doppelganger's words.

Was it true? Was I doomed to be haunted?

"You're a monster!" I roared menacingly, with enough intensity to strain the blood vessels in my eyes. "You took everything from me for no good reason."

"I'm a monster? I did nothing you did not already do to yourself," the figure scoffed. "Now, alone on the promontory's edge, you flee like a coward from your punishment."

"I did everything I could to save Beatrice," I muttered, shaking my head in disbelief.

I glared at the figure as it turned away and chuckled morbidly at the events transpiring. Then, the air around me suddenly felt heavier, and its piercing, inhuman gaze stole my attention. A sudden realization dawned on me as I stood there, wrestling with my thoughts and emotions. The doppelganger was right—I could not run away from myself, my past, or my most persistent insecurities. However, I did not have to face them alone; I had loved ones who cared about me and would support me no matter what.

Taking a deep breath, I turned to face the doppelganger once more, but this time with newfound courage.

"You may be a part of me, but you don't define me," I said, steadfast. "I may have flaws and struggles, but I am a good person. I will face you head-on."

"It was always a fool, always a great fool," the doppelganger began as if reciting an ancient text. "It stands before me and carries itself as the god it never could be. It led to a wasted life, marred by its own unwillingness to accept the limitations nature bound to it. There was beauty there, indeed, yet it submitted to the beast inside.

"Not all was lost, though," it continued, taking a step forward with a rising intensity in its voice. "The beast has been freed, yes, but the beautiful soul has likewise been liberated from its carceral fate. It—the fool—is free! It will do as it will do, like an actor reciting his lines in the spotlight. Fools like it cannot deviate from the script—imbue the performance with individuality, make it their own. Though a life spent on a rehearsed, predetermined voyage is tragic, the tragedy ends tonight, swiftly and definitively."

I prepared myself to attack the shadowy figure. Meanwhile, it prepared itself for me.

"Show me what sort of hell you can bring down upon me!" the doppelganger snapped as it charged forward to strike me.

The doppelganger knocked me to the ground with a wild haymaker before kicking me in the ribs. Reeling in pain, I dodged the next blow to regain my footing. I charged at the shadowy figure and tackled it to the ground. It swung at my head, connecting its balled fist with my left temple. Dazed, I attempted to block the next hit but failed; it toppled me over with another mighty punch to my cheek. Stunned on the ground, I felt two hands ferociously wrap around my neck like two inexorable pythons and begin to squeeze the life out of me.

The more I struggled, the more harshly I was punished. A strident ringing started in my ears as I stared at the two empty voids where the figure's eyes should have been. With each passing second, I steadily began to lose consciousness: the world around me becoming grayer. Just before darkness completely consumed my vision, the doppelganger stopped and snickered.

"Such a tragic fool," it scornfully declared as it dragged me by the arm to the edge of the promontory. "Let's finish this."

With that, I felt my body rise into the air before hurtling toward the stones in the water below. Time and space moved slowly as I fell from atop the promontory toward a watery grave. Narrowly avoiding the large, minacious rocks, I entered the water with such force that I could not breathe for a few seconds, smaller stones slicing my skin. The pummeling currents beneath the water's surface immediately whipped me against the rocks. Desperate to get above the surface, I flailed with my arms and legs, finally emerging and gasping violently for air.

I screamed, flushing some of the stygian water from my crippled throat. I frantically searched for a way to leverage myself so I could figure out my next move. After reorienting myself, I turned toward the promontory where the shadowy figure stood, staring maliciously at me. Its eyes and mine met as I grappled fruitlessly against the raging waters of the sea. I was immobilized by its gaze; I could not even twitch a muscle out of synchronicity with him. My body grew weak as the waves savagely struck me over and over.

What is the meaning of this? I thought, sinking under the water once again.

With the last remaining energy I could muster, I forced my way out of the depths one more time. As my head found its way to the air again, I now noticed something different atop the promontory: two other figures standing beside the doppelganger.

Who are you?

Even from a distance, they seemed very familiar to me.

"Beatrice? Dr. Altamura?" I whispered, unable to project my voice enough for anyone else to hear.

Looking at the figures of the two people I loved most, I managed a gasp of air as a sense of realization slipped into place.

I think I understand what I need to do.

I dove into the water and allowed the currents to carry my body wherever they would. I closed my eyes and let go: let go of all physical resistance, let go of all emotion. Soon, I could not feel anything around me as I drifted into the water's murky depths. I had found a strange peacefulness within this space, one I had not had in so long. I relinquished control, and in return, quietude was my reward, unlike anything from this planet.

"You're back with us!" A woman exclaimed from beside me, her voice quavering. "Open your eyes."

I complied, opening my eyes and seeing that I was back on top of the promontory. I briefly glimpsed the shadowy figure struggling against the waves where I had been just moments ago. The fiend cried out in fear as the pernicious waves engulfed it for the last time. My legs felt exceedingly weak as I attempted to step back, and I lost my balance before stumbling backward onto the ground.

I breathed deeply and slowly in an attempt to re-center myself, completely overwhelmed by what had just occurred. Out of my peripheral vision, I noticed two figures coming around my sides to sit in front of me. They wore loose-fitting clothing the color of glacial ice that draped over them like Ancient Greeks. As my eyes tracked up to their faces, I was wonderstruck by the immediate familiarity of their features. Rendered completely speechless, all I could do was stare at them for several seconds.

"Beatrice! Dr. Altamura!" I blurted out, overcome by the bliss of seeing them again. "I don't understand how this is possible. You both are dead."

"All of this will make more sense later," Dr. Altamura said softly, beaming down at me. "You're a good person who did everything possible for us."

"We love you," Beatrice chimed in, kneeling at my side and embracing me.

I could not believe what I was experiencing. Dr. Altamura and Beatrice, two people who had been such an important part of my life, were here in front of me—speaking to me as if nothing had happened. As I hugged Beatrice back, I choked up. It felt so real, so heartening to have them here with me once again.

"But how?" I finally managed to ask as I held Beatrice at arm's length to look at her. "How is this possible?"

Dr. Altamura smiled gently.

"There are things in this world that we can't always explain. But what matters is that we are here with you now."

I took a deep breath, trying to process everything that was happening. My senses seemed dull in this moment I shared with Dr. Altamura and Beatrice; I felt no pain and did not feel cold despite my grievous plunge into the sea. It was like a beautiful dream from which I never wanted to wake up. I stared at my loved ones and saw that they looked just like they had when they were alive and healthy. Whether real or not, Dr. Altamura and Beatrice were here with me.

"We are here to guide you," Beatrice said, her voice soothing and soft. "We are here to help you navigate this journey you are on, to get past the treacherous waters from which you just escaped."

Much like when I was underwater, serenity graced me once again: a feeling of being truly cared for and understood. Dr. Altamura and Beatrice had always been there for me when I needed them, and now, even in death, they were still by my side.

"Thank you," I whispered, my voice filled with gratitude. "Thank you for being here."

Dr. Altamura and Beatrice smiled at me, a clear and pure expression of their love and reassurance. I embraced them one last time.

"You were the best friend I could have ever asked for," Beatrice murmured into my ear as my arms encircled her.

Being with them was like I had gone to a paradise high above the clouds—up into the Empyrean. For a moment, embracing Beatrice made me believe I was there; it was the only way I could see these brief candles that had been snuffed out far too soon on this unjust plane of existence. But then I noticed subtle signs of my body's physical distress: the soreness of my feet, the aching in my neck, the tiredness of my eyes. Accounting for these various sensations grounded me more, giving me a much clearer sense of where I was.

"Wait," I slowly backed up from them. "You said you 'are here to guide' me. Are you coming with me?"

"In a sense," Dr. Altamura answered, placing a strong hand on my shoulder. "Just not in the way you think we can. No harm has befallen you; your incarcerated demons failed to exact their final vengeance on you. You still have a chance: seek out help for these demons. Fix the broken vessel. If the doppelganger reappears, we may be powerless to its fury."

The gravity of the situation crashed upon me like a large stone. Making eye contact with Dr. Altamura, the vaguely pained look on his face conveyed meaning beyond his words. I rubbed my neck, attending to my body again to confirm what he told me. I squeezed their hands in mine, heartbroken that I would need to leave. I nodded at my companions and then headed back toward the trail without another word. No matter where Beatrice and Dr. Altamura were, I knew I had their support—I knew I could heal from the trauma of losing them.

CHAPTER TWENTY

Departure

The light of midmorning was a cruel reminder that peaceful slumber was often too short, especially for the unrested mind. I held my eyes tightly shut before conceding and opening them slowly, allowing my blurry vision to resolve. As my vision cleared up, I took in the unexciting sight of a matte white wall upon which an equally bland clock hung. This initial glimpse of my surroundings did not ring a bell, but then the sudden realization that I was not in my home gripped me. I sluggishly raised my head to close the open blinds that were permitting the sun to mock me from its celestial perch high above the world. Clearing my throat of phlegm that had accumulated overnight, I grasped the sides of my bed to prop myself up so I could examine the room, remembering now where I was.

The tragedy of losing Beatrice in such an unexpected and devastating manner last year was a harsh reminder of the dangers lurking behind the curtains of routine healthcare operations. It also underlined the essential, often-overlooked role of behavioral support services that physicians frequently eschew out of fear of being judged and stripped of their licenses. After the events at the promontory, it was clear to me that I needed to break this cycle and get help; I knew that was why Dr. Altamura and Beatrice had appeared before me.

The nightmares had become irrepressible: their guilt-ridden scenes suffocating my heart. That same evening, after making it back to my car safely, I drove to Alta Vista Hospital and presented to the emergency department for a psychiatric evaluation. The nurse at the front desk took one look at me and knew something was wrong. She led me to a room where I sat on the edge of the bed, my hands shaking, waiting for someone to come and assess me.

As I lay back in my bed, I examined my torso and limbs, searching for the injuries I remembered sustaining when that dark fiend hurled me off the promontory. I was shocked when I found nothing but healthy, intact skin. Not a scratch anywhere on me.

Did any of that really happen? I started to question my grasp of reality. *I guess my clothes weren't wet when I drove over here. All of it felt so real, but then again, I would probably be dead if it were.*

"I hope it's okay that I come to visit you," I heard someone say from the doorway of my exam room.

Dr. Coffman came in and sat down across from me, his presence alleviating my disordered internal environment.

"Dr. Coffman," I said, hunched over from lassitude. "It's good to see you. I'm sorry it has to be under less-than-ideal circumstances."

"Do you want to talk about it?" he posed the question hesitantly, seemingly worried he would upset me. "Don't feel pressured to do so."

I took him up on his offer, diving into the details of the shadowy figure, the altercation, my near-death experience, the appearance of Beatrice and Dr. Altamura, and the epiphany about my need for mental healthcare. In the back of my mind, I was cognizant that this unfiltered revelation to Dr. Coffman could affect my standing in the residency, regardless of what our accrediting body's guidelines said. But I did not care; he needed to know. Besides, I trusted Dr. Coffman and his judgment.

"You've gone through a lot today," he sympathized, nodding slowly toward the floor with downcast eyes. "I'm so proud of you for having such deep insight into your health needs. You know what they say: we make the worst patients. Fortunately, you defied that stereotype and got what you needed. Don't worry about anything with the program; we will fully support and accommodate you to make sure you get everything you need."

He's a good man, I thought as I thanked him, looking deeply into his eyes to convey the extent of my trust.

As we finished connecting over my recent issues, a loud series of knocking caught my ear.

"Good morning, you all." A young man—maybe a year older than me—set foot into the room. "Dr. Coffman, it's a pleasure to see you."

"Likewise, Marvin," he replied, rising to his feet promptly. "I'll give you some space so that you can properly evaluate your patient."

With that, Dr. Coffman patted my shoulder gingerly as he exited the room.

The young man introduced himself as Dr. Marvin Belardo, the psychiatrist working on the inpatient behavioral health unit. He noted he had recently been hired to replace one of the older psychiatrists who retired a few months ago. He had a kind face, his eyes filled with empathy and understanding, similar to Dr. Price's. He listened as I poured my heart out, summarizing the events at the promontory and the other issues I told Dr. Coffman.

After what felt like hours, Dr. Belardo spoke, his words gentle and measured. He told me that I was not alone and that there were people who cared about me—who wanted to help. He recommended an inpatient admission for intensive management, a safe place where I could focus on my mental health and healing. I agreed, knowing deep down that I needed this. I could not continue to suffer in silence as so many of my brothers and sisters did every day.

Staring at the blank white walls, I reoriented myself, realizing I was in my room in the behavioral health unit. The next few days were a blur of therapy sessions, medication adjustments, and moments of clarity where I could finally begin to process what had happened and start repairing the vessel's cracks. In his typical benevolent manner, Dr. Coffman came to check on me almost every day—his presence a small but appreciated gesture of goodwill. Through his actions, he reassured me that I was never alone in this journey to recovery. After four days, I was discharged, feeling much more stable than when I had initially presented to the emergency department. The group and individual therapy sessions had helped, and the psychotropic medications had begun to work their magic. I had a long road ahead of me; recovery was not confined to my time in the inpatient behavioral health unit. All the same, I felt like I had a fighting chance for the first time in months.

I entrusted Soraya and Vincent with the information about my hospitalization, and they planned to visit me today to see how things were going. Hearing the doorbell ring, I marched energetically over to the door to see my two best friends and co-residents standing outside. Vincent's arms were full of paper bags and drinks from a Greek restaurant we all loved, and Soraya brought over a large casserole dish filled to the brim with my favorite dessert. I invited them in, and we sat down in the dining room to have lunch together.

"How have you been doing, brother?" Vincent asked me, exuding genuine concern.

"Better and better every day," I answered, patting him on the shoulder. "I can't tell you how glad I am to see you both."

"We've missed you so much," Soraya said. "I'm just so glad you're doing better. I know you've gone through a lot lately."

As we sat around the dining room table, enjoying the delicious Greek cuisine and homemade dessert, I felt grateful for the support system I had in my life. These two individuals had been there for me through thick and thin, always ready to offer a safe spot to land, a listening ear, or simply a comforting presence. Vincent, with his easy smile and infectious laughter, was always the life of the party. He had a way of making even the darkest moments seem a little brighter. Soraya, with her quiet strength and unwavering loyalty, was like a rock that I could always rely on.

I took a deep breath, trying to compose myself as I prepared to address the elephant in the room.

"I just can't shake this feeling that I could've done something more for Bea. She was like family to us. I was supposed to protect her, but I failed."

Vincent reached over and squeezed my shoulder, presenting a nonjudgmental smile.

"You did everything you could; that's all anyone could have asked for. You can't blame yourself for things that were out of your control."

Soraya nodded in agreement, her eyes filled with compassion.

"We all carry guilt in situations like these, but we have to remember that we're only human. We can't control everything that happens in life despite our best efforts. Altamura taught us that."

I wiped away some stray tears, feeling relieved. For so long, I had been carrying this burden of responsibility, blaming myself for Beatrice's tragic fate. But now, with the support of my friends, I was finally internalizing that I could not change the past. All I could do was honor Beatrice's memory and learn from the experience.

"Thank you both," I said, my voice a rasp. "I needed to get that off my chest, and I'm so grateful to have you both here."

Vincent and Soraya encircled me tightly with their arms, giving me desperately needed solace. At that moment, I felt disencumbered and much lighter in my seat.

As we ate and chatted, the conversation turned to our time together as residents at the hospital and clinic. We reminisced about the long hours, the challenging clinical cases, and the bond we had formed during these past three years. Soraya and Vincent shared stories of their struggles and triumphs, reminding me that each of us had experienced unique obstacles during training. After lunch, we moved to the living room, where we spent the afternoon catching up on our lives outside of work. Vincent told us tales of his latest escapades, while Soraya described her recent adventures on weekend day trips and photography. It was a welcome distraction from the monotony of my recovery, and I found myself laughing and smiling more than I had in weeks.

As the sun began to set and the day drew to a close, I felt shrouded in a cocoon of contentment. In the presence of my two dear friends, all the pain and uncertainty of the past few weeks seemed to fade away. As they prepared to leave, Soraya and Vincent gathered their things and stood at the door, ready to bid me farewell.

"We'll be back soon, brother," Vincent turned to me with a smile and said. "We'll get through this together."

With those words echoing in my ears, I knew that, no matter what challenges lay ahead, my friends were ready to support me every step of the way. With that thought in mind, I realized

I could face whatever the future held with strength, courage, and the unwavering bond of friendship that had carried me through this rite of passage in our medical careers. Now that I was in a better headspace, I decided it was time to revisit my scrapbook. I dusted it off and spent the rest of the evening recalling the good times.

On the day before our residency graduation, all eleven residents in the program gathered together at a park with a large pavilion for a cookout and group celebration of the soon-to-be graduates. The aroma of grilled hamburgers, mushrooms, and lemon pepper-dusted chicken filled the air as we eagerly awaited Dr. Calisto's arrival, our guest of honor. Dr. Calisto had been in leadership when many of us started the residency program, and he was a mentor and friend to many of us. He guided us through the ups and downs of our training, bestowing his wisdom when we needed it most. As we saw him approaching the pavilion, ebullience surged through the group.

We—the third-year residents who had trained under Dr. Calisto—were particularly excited to see him. We had a close bond with him, and his presence at the cookout warmed our hearts as little else could. As the festivities began, we exchanged silly gifts, exchanged uplifting stories, and toasted each other. We reminisced about every step of the journey, retreading similar grounds that the third-years had trodden the other day while still finding new memories to uncover. Laughter filled the air, and the camaraderie among us was palpable.

Dr. Calisto regaled us with stories from his days as a resident and offered us words of encouragement and advice for the future. His presence reminded us of the importance of mentorship in the medical field, and we were grateful we had him as a guiding force in our lives.

The next day, we three graduates rode to the Mariner's Inn, a fancy establishment in the heart of Frieden Bay. The sun shone even more brightly than the day before, casting a warm glow over the cobblestone pathways leading to the entrance. The inn's grounds opened into a wondrous courtyard with vibrant flowers, herbs, and other plants, giving the air a sweet and fragrant scent. As we ambulated over to the ballroom where the ceremony would be held, we bantered back and forth, telling funny and touching stories.

Dr. Mose was our master of ceremony for the event. She greeted us warmly with a twinkle in her eyes, her fiery red hair framing her proud face. After family and friends filed in, joined the graduates at tables across the ballroom, and took their seats, Dr. Mose launched into her introduction and formally welcomed everyone in attendance, which set the tone for the emotional and uplifting ceremony that was to come. The room was decorated beautifully, with floral centerpieces adorning the tables and soft music playing in the background. As the ceremony began, Dr. Mose played a video to commemorate and celebrate the life and legacy of Beatrice, our beloved friend and co-resident. The video was a fitting tribute to her, showcasing her vibrant personality and the impact she had on all of us during her time in the program.

Tears flowed freely from many of us as we watched. Through my tear-soaked eyes, I stared long at the images on the screen as they came and went. This was the woman I knew so well. Seeing her greatness memorialized before us stung me like a needle dripping with sorrow, but this moment also gave me the closure I needed. I pictured myself standing on the promontory with Dr. Altamura and her, and in my mental recreation of them, I saw their forms dematerialize around me. Peace settled on my soul as I felt the warmth of the sun and the coolness of the air in that place.

After a moment of silence to remember Beatrice, Dr. Mose recognized each of the graduates individually—sharing anecdotes about our time as residents and our growth during their training. As she spoke about each of us, I could feel a swell of pride for all we had accomplished and all that was yet to come. The ceremony was a mix of laughter and tears, of memories shared and of dreams for the future. As we stood together, our framed completion certificates in hand, we knew this was a new beginning. We had been through so much together: faced challenges, relished victories big and small, and came out stronger and more resilient.

As we walked out of the ballroom, I finally felt proud. Proud of navigating the challenges of family medicine residency training. Proud of making the lives of patients and colleagues better. Proud of all of the work that led to my relocation to Frieden Bay. Proud of having known Dr. Altamura and Beatrice. Proud of doing everything I could for Beatrice. Proud of overcoming my demons. Proud of restoring this broken vessel to its former glory.

For the first time since I initially arrived in Frieden Bay, I strode down the circuitous hallway leading to Mr. Haron's office to drop off my apartment keys. Vincent offered to keep my belongings, and movers had already picked up my large furniture to move it back to my hometown. As I walked along the winding walls, I realized how much brighter the hallway looked. Even though I did not notice a difference in the lighting itself, my vision was clearer, and within a few moments, I reached the enormous door of the landlord's office—untouched by time.

"Come in," Mr. Haron called immediately after I knocked. "Ah! It's you! How are you doing today?"

"I'm doing well," I answered. "My friends and I are about to take a trip, so I wanted to return these."

Mr. Haron reached out his large hand to accept the keys. He looked down at them with an almost pensive look overtaking his brow.

"I hope you found your time here in Frieden Bay worthwhile," he said softly. "It was a pleasure having you as a tenant. I have no doubt that Dr. Altamura would be over the moon if he could see you today."

I nodded slowly and lowered my head in quiet reflection.

"As you cross over to your new life, do not lose your reason for practicing medicine. Take the lessons you learned and serve your community."

I nodded confidently, thanked Mr. Haron, and shook his hand before taking my leave from the strange administrative building. It was time to meet up with Vincent and Soraya.

The three of us had been inseparable since we started residency. And now, after years of hard work and perseverance, we were finally graduating from residency. It was time to celebrate, and what better way to do so than by embarking on a camping trip in the rugged mountains outside of Frieden Bay? As soon as we arrived at the base of the mountain range, the freedom of the great outdoors flowed through us. The crisp mountain air filled our lungs, and nature's vast expanse stretched before us, beckoning us to explore. With our backpacks loaded with supplies for this long-awaited trip, we began the ascent to our base camp.

The hike was challenging, but we tackled it enthusiastically, lending a hand wherever necessary to make sure nobody was left behind. We pushed ourselves to our limits, navigating the rocky terrain. As we reached the summit, the marvelous beauty of the landscape took our breath away. The sun descended in the sky, emitting golden light over the rugged peaks and deep valleys far below us. We stood in awe of the majesty of nature, feeling small and insignificant in the grand scheme of the world.

That night, we gathered around a crackling bonfire, the flames swaying and flickering in the nearly impenetrable inkiness of the night. We shared stories and laughter, reminiscing about our medical training and looking forward to what lay down the line. We talked about our future career plans, including Vincent's move to Denver to work as a full-time hospitalist, Soraya's position as a full-spectrum family physician in a rural community similar to Oktusha, and my new job as an outpatient clinician back in my hometown. At that moment, surrounded by the mountains and the heat of the fire, I was happy. I knew we would always have each other no matter where life took us. As friends. As colleagues. And as kindred spirits.

In the light of the bonfire, I looked closely at Vincent and Soraya, their faces illuminated by the flames. It felt surreal to remember what the three of us looked like when we first started this chapter of our lives. Vincent, with his ever-messy hair but neatly-groomed beard, and Soraya, always poised, her hijab immaculately styled, a contrast to her often-furrowed brow signaling deep thought during clinical work. Then there was me, perpetually clutching my coffee as a shield against the chaos of a hospital that never slept.

As I stared into the fire, I remembered how we would joke around with our medical assistants, bring in treats to enjoy with everyone, and have philosophical discussions about healthcare during our didactic sessions. We grew from naïve interns—fumbling through our first procedures—into competent physicians, confident in our skills but still espousing the humility that medicine relentlessly teaches us.

"I'm so glad we met each other," I said, breaking the silence and looking at my friends intently. "I don't know where I'd be without you all. You all made this journey possible."

Soraya smiled softly and nodded.

"We got through some tough times, didn't we? I can't imagine having done this without you guys."

Vincent let out a low chuckle, throwing another log onto the bonfire, sending a shower of sparks into the night sky.

"Remember the twenty-four-hour shifts during the influenza surge back when we were interns? I thought I was going to collapse right there on the wards."

"And you almost did," I added, sincere laughter blending with the crackle of the fire. "But Soraya found you asleep, slumped in a chair in the first-floor lobby."

Soraya's phone buzzed, and she glanced at it before tucking it back in her pocket.

"Another job offer after I've already signed my contract," she said with a chuckle. "I would say I'm flattered if it weren't for the constant barrage of emails."

Vincent pulled out several cans of our favorite local IPA from his massive backpack and made sure we each had one.

"To us," he toasted, lifting his can of ale high. "For surviving and thriving."

We bumped our cans together in our solitary celebration and sipped our surprisingly cool IPAs. The road had been rough, marked by sleepless nights and heartbreaking decisions, but it had led us to this perfect night where the past intertwined with the present. We had started as strangers, bound only by our commitment to heal. Now, we were more than colleagues, more than friends. We were a tribe, shaped by the blazing fires of residency, forever linked by our journey through the most arduous and rewarding years of our lives.

Under the twinkling gaze of the universe, we related more stories and memories until the fire burned down to glowing embers. Through it all, our bond remained as steady as the enduring flames, a promise of inextricably linked destinies in the many challenges and triumphs yet to come.

"I love you all," I said, looking each of them in the eye. "You are some of the greatest people I have ever met."

As we lay under the starry sky, we listened to the mountain breeze moving through the trees, gently rattling the branches and rustling the leaves. We had this glorious opportunity to slow down, decompress, and re-center ourselves after the whirlwind of the past three years. Our camping trip had been just what we needed: a chance to connect more deeply with nature, ourselves, and each other. I drifted off to sleep in my cozy tent, listening to the crickets chirping in the night.

CHAPTER TWENTY-ONE

A Brisk Morning Breeze

The wispy rays of the rising sun reflected off of the windshield of a sedan whose driver calmly adjusted the volume knob of the radio to bring the sound of classic rock music to an easily audible level. I rested my head on my open left hand and used my right hand to keep the vehicle moving straight along the highway I took daily to work. After exiting the highway and stopping at a traffic light, I grabbed my iced coffee. I sipped at it before proceeding to the two-story red-brick building where our community-based ambulatory clinic operated.

The beginning of July signaled the arrival of new physicians in communities across the country and many parts of the world. Reviewing the roster of our first cohort of residents again last week made me smile from ear to ear, reminding me of starting my training nine years ago. As the Program Director of the new Virgil Altamura Memorial Family Medicine Residency, I had been eagerly anticipating their arrival for many months, knowing the impact they would have on the patients we served every day.

My phone vibrated in the cupholder just before I parked my car.

"Happy first day of the program, Mr. Big Shot! Want to talk before you get started?" the message read.

Before I could formulate a response, an incoming video call made my phone buzz in my hand. Vincent's huge grin rapidly engulfed my phone screen; his face was way too close to the camera as he fumbled with his phone. As he moved it back, I immediately noticed how much he had changed since we last saw each other. His once-tousled black hair was now neatly styled, and he'd shaved his beard, leaving his face clean-shaven. Despite the physical changes, his eyes still sparkled with the same amiable glint I remembered well.

"Vin!" I exclaimed, unable to contain my excitement.

"Well, look who it is!" he said, his grin widening. "I haven't seen you in so long, brother! How have you been?"

"I've been very well. I was just trying to text you back."

"Have you talked with Soraya recently?"

"No," I shook my head. "She's been so busy with her new job."

"I know," Vincent responded, a flicker of disappointment passing across his face. "Last we spoke, she mentioned she wanted to get together in New York for our new conference.

She has had her hands so full as the Chief Medical Officer of that large clinic system up in Minnesota."

I learned that Vincent was working at a federally qualified health center in New Mexico, providing medical care to underserved communities. He and his wife Claudia recently welcomed their first child, a beautiful baby girl named Iris. Vincent's face lit up as he spoke about his daughter, and I could see the pride and joy in his eyes. In addition to his work at the health center, Vincent also spent time delivering babies at a major hospital in Albuquerque. He spoke passionately about the miracles he witnessed daily, the joy of bringing new life into the world, and the importance of providing quality care to mothers and babies. I joked with him that I would have never pegged him as an obstetrician but that I was proud of him for exemplifying our specialty.

"When you have time, I would love to get you out to New Mexico so you can spend time with my family and me," he said spiritedly. "I could show you so many cool things around the area. The high desert of the northern part of the state is unlike anything you have ever encountered."

"For sure! And I would love to schedule you for a lecture with our residents. They could learn a lot from you."

My phone vibrated with a new message notification.

"Our Program Manager is texting me about some things she needs before the residents get here," I remarked, glancing at my push notifications.

"I guess that's our cue," Vincent stated, frowning slightly.

Even over the virtual platform, Vincent and I looked at each other and had a moment of mute reflection. We both became glassy-eyed as we looked at one another, basking in this wondrous moment of connection and companionship.

"It was good seeing and talking to you again," he finally said. "You get in there and give those young docs the training they deserve."

"It was good seeing you again, brother. I miss you," I told Vincent, my eyes scrunched from a pang of longing. "We'll talk again very soon."

Emerging from my vehicle, I immediately appreciated the lovely presence of a brisk morning breeze. Half a dozen medical assistants greeted me as they filed in for a pre-clinic huddle before kicking off the workday. I marched across the parking lot, delivering my usual morning pleasantries like someone did for me years ago. After topping off my insulated metal cup with fresh coffee, I headed to my office and set my laptop bag next to my vast swivel chair.

Sitting comfortably at my desk, I completed forms for our new residency program. As Program Director, I had to make sure everything was in order before our first batch of residents officially started. I had been doing paperwork for many months, and these forms were for final verification of the funding we used from one of our grants to start the program and convert the old software development building into a fully functional primary care clinic.

Getting this program off the ground was hectic but very much worth it. As a prime example of the madness, the first interview season was wild; we had received hundreds of applications from aspiring physicians and medical graduates eager to join our program. It took my colleagues and me almost two weeks to send out our interview invitations because the caliber of our applicants had floored us. In addition to recruiting excellent residency applicants, we managed to attract top-notch faculty and secure partnerships with leading hospitals in the area. I was confident we would soon be one of the country's premier family medicine residency programs. All we needed to do was stay on track and continue doing great work.

As I was about to send the completed paperwork to the administrative office, my phone rang.

"Are we all set for the residents to start their orientation in a few hours?" Dr. Shivansh Patel, our most senior core faculty member and Associate Program Director, inquired.

"Everything's in order: I finished the paperwork and orientation schedule for the entire month. We're ready to welcome our new folks with open arms," I assured him.

"Great to hear. I'm looking forward to meeting them. I have a good feeling about this group," Dr. Patel chirped.

After I hung up the phone, I contemplated how our program was about to commence its first chapter, which simultaneously provoked excitement and uncertainty. No matter how I felt inside, I needed to exercise strong leadership and project confidence. I needed to serve as the resolute captain of this new vessel on the turbulent sea. Within the next two hours, the new residents arrived, eager and appropriately nervous, ready to begin their journey in family medicine. Each new physician had a look of cautious optimism in their eyes, which reminded me of how I was when I started my journey. After our four interns made it inside our conference room and took a seat at the table, I stepped forward to welcome them.

"Good morning, everyone," I started, reminding myself of Dr. Calisto and his spirited way of speaking. "I'm honored to see you all again today. A lot of time has passed since I interviewed you all, and I can tell you that, despite the time, I still clearly recall the promise each of you brings to the field of family medicine."

Looking at the small group, I clearly remembered each resident physician's defining attributes. There was Gloria Rose, the daughter of a well-known cardiologist and epidemiologist. She completed her public health training while balancing it with the demands of medical school coursework. There was Hikaru Tamaki, a Japanese immigrant who earned a doctoral degree in biochemistry before completing medical school in Tokyo. Hikaru impressively infused his biochemistry expertise into his work as a medical student, creating research opportunities for his peers. There was Daren Peshlakai, a tall and slender Diné man who pursued medicine as his second career after working as an architectural consultant for many years. He was also a prolific writer, publishing three books of poetry—one in his native tongue—all within five years.

Then, there was Fernando Portinari, a tall man with dark features in his mid-twenties. It had been years since I last saw him, and back then, it had been fairly brief and at an inauspicious time. His dark brown hair and the subtle roundness of the tip of his nose reminded me of someone who had meant so much to me. Though I had an undeniable connection to him because of Beatrice, Fernando was a remarkable young physician who had been inducted into the Alpha Omega Alpha Honor Medical Society and Gold Humanism Honor Society for his excellent performance in his basic and clinical science coursework. If his sister were still with us, she would be incredibly proud of him and his accomplishments.

"My name is Dr. Dante Allegro, and I am your Program Director," I announced. "I am confident you will all find your training here in our program outstanding. Your faculty and I have been planning your curriculum for over two years, putting a lot of thought into every facet."

For the remainder of the day, I introduced the residents to all of the faculty, staff, and ancillary personnel at the clinic and hospitals. As we walked over to the clinical staff services office in one of the hospitals for the residents to get their identification badges, I imagined that Beatrice and Dr. Altamura followed us, rooting for the residents as the heart and soul of our residency program. We passed a mirror on the way, and in it, I imagined Dr. Calisto staring back at me with my younger self behind him. Each of those people inspired me in ways that they could not possibly fathom.

The next day, I returned to my office early in the morning to finish some work before I left for a conference in Florida. A thump at my door broke my concentration.

"Please, come in," I called.

A dark-haired and dark-eyed head poked around the edge of the door. Fernando stepped into my office.

"Fernando, it's a pleasure to see you again," I exclaimed as I approached him and reached for his hand to shake.

"Dr. Allegro, it's so great to see you again, too!" he exclaimed, his timidity melting away. "I'm sorry to barge in like this. Before we get started with everything today, I wanted to see if we could talk."

"Absolutely," I replied, returning to my chair and gesturing to an open chair in front of my desk. "What do you have on your mind?"

"Bea always spoke so highly of you when we would talk with me on the phone or visit over the holidays," Fernando said, settling into the chair. "She thought the world of you. Knowing my interest in pursuing medicine when I was still in college, she always told me that I would be lucky to be under the tutelage of someone like you."

As Fernando told me all of this, I was speechless. I cast my gaze at a faded photograph on my desk of my co-residents and me.

"She was always so humble and kind-hearted. I respected her greatly," I said, grinning with each word.

"I would like for you to be my advisor and mentor, Dr. Allegro," Fernando concisely stated, getting straight to the point. "That would mean so much to my family and me."

"I would be happy to do that for you," I agreed, leaning closer to him.

Seeing Fernando sitting across from me reminded me of all the beautiful times with Beatrice. After she died, I was a lost and broken man, entrenched in depression and trauma. Even from beyond, she protected me and gave me the power to carry on, to become a better and stronger person.

"What was my sister like when she was a resident?" he asked, his voice filled with emotion. "If you don't mind my asking, that is."

I took a deep breath, trying to hold back my tears as memories of Beatrice inundated my mind.

"Your sister was amazing," I began. "She was not just a talented clinician but also a natural leader. Her patients loved her, and she always went above and beyond to make sure they received the best care possible."

As I spoke, I could see the pain and longing in Fernando's eyes. It was clear how much he missed his sister and how deeply her loss had affected him all these years later. Throughout our conversation, I shared several stories of Beatrice's time as a resident. I told Fernando about when she stayed late into the night to help a patient in need and how she always went out of her way to mentor younger residents and medical students. With each story, Fernando's eyes lit up with hints of pride and sadness shining through.

Despite the heavy subject matter, I sensed a connection as we talked about Beatrice. It was as if her spirit was present in that moment, guiding us through our grief and reminding us of the love and light she had brought into our lives. As our conversation came to an end, Fernando thanked me for telling him things he never knew about his sister. It was a bittersweet reminder of the love and loss we had experienced together. But it was also a testament to the resilience and strength that Beatrice had instilled in both of us.

"She would be overjoyed if she could see you here today," I remarked, showing Fernando the way to the first orientation activity of the day.

"Bea would feel the same about you," he replied, glowing with new happiness and hope that raised both of our spirits into the sky like beautiful albatrosses soaring over a perfect sea.